THE TOTALLY UNAUTHORIZED ENRON® JOKE BOOK™

Created, Collected and Edited

by

Tim Barry

TOTALLY
The♥ Unauthorized Enron Joke Book

Table of Contents

✱ ✱ ✱

TOTALLY
The Unauthorized Enron Joke Book

"The Human race has one really effective weapon and that is laughter" – Mark Twain

1.0   Introduction

Enron's meteoric rise from an obscure Houston based pipeline company to the seventh largest company in the United States pretty much guaranteed that anything it did would be noticed. Unfortunately, becoming the largest bankruptcy in the history of U.S. business was probably not the kind of attention that Enron management had in mind. And, as is often the case, notoriety has lead in turn to the attention (usually unwanted!!) of humorists and critics. The Enron disaster is just plain too big, too expensive and, well, too visible to not make a really great target for jokes of all sizes and shapes.

This is a collection of humor about Enron. The company. The shareholders. Politicians. The auditors. Consultants. Ex-CEO Ken Lay and his executive team. Jokes, mock news stories, top 10 lists, poems, songs and more. Most of these have never been published before. Many of the items are laced with appearances by famous people from current events to further liven up the material.

Each chapter takes humorous aim at a different aspect of the Enron debacle:

> To get started, **"Enron Potpourri"** has a little of everything – some management, some politics, some accounting, some executives, etc.

> **"Investors and Investments"** takes a whack at the reports, the offshore investment partnerships and other things contributing to this shareholder nightmare.

> **"Executives and Consultants"** takes a topsy turvy look at the brain trust that should have kept Enron on track to bigger and better things.

> **"Accounting and Auditing"** pokes fun at the folks who were supposed to be keeping track of the chips.

"Politics and Politicians" casts a jaundiced eye on the basic question Enron and every other business has asked for years: "Is the only good politician a 'paid for' politician?"

"Ken Lay and his Crew" takes a look at the guy at the top and some of the other people who were running the show at Enron.

The bonus chapter, **"Enron Late Night"** features the best of the quips and one liners from news and the late night talk shows.

"Dramatis Personae" lists the famous folks who are mentioned throughout the book and where they appear.

We hope everyone (maybe even some former Enron employees and shareholders) will enjoy this eclectic collection of humorous material and view it not as mean spirited but rather in the true tradition of Jonathon Swift, Sinclair Lewis, *Mad Magazine*, *National Lampoon* and other purveyors of parody and satire, namely using humor to prod at the hubris, foibles and fumbles of events and those involved in them.

✱ ✱ ✱

Ed. Note: We didn't kill Enron - don't blame us!! It was dead when we got there. If you don't think a business disaster of this magnitude is the least bit humorous, on one level we're probably in violent agreement. Lots of people lost jobs, money, and more in what's probably going to turn out to be a pretty sordid scandal. Ugly stuff.

On the other hand, there is no point in crying over spilled stock, either and sometimes humor can make a point far better than a room full of lawyers or politicians. And laughter, if not the best, is certainly a good medicine. Take a look inside - we may not be able to make you forget the unpleasant reality that Enron represents but we think we may be able to convince you to at least smile at it a little.

2.0   Enron Potpourri

If Ken Lay had been the Captain of the Titanic he would have told the passengers, "Don't worry - we're just stopping to take on ice!"

✳ ✳ ✳

Q.   What's the difference between Enron and a religious cult?

A.   The holy books of religious cults are not audited by Arthur Andersen.

✳ ✳ ✳

Advice from an attorney to an ex-Enron employee about to testify before a Congressional committee: "You have the right to remain silent. Anything you say can and will be misquoted and then used against you."

✳ ✳ ✳

Q.   What do you get if you cross the prospectus for an Enron offshore partnership with the Godfather?

A.   An offering you can't understand.

✳ ✳ ✳

> An Enron exec name of Skilling
> Testified to the Senate quite willing.
> What he stated, alas
> Tried to cover his ass
> And made the day's hearings less thrilling.

✳ ✳ ✳

We have been unable to confirm the rumor that Motorola and Enron were contemplating a merger just prior to Enron's demise. The combined entity would have been named:

MORON

✳ ✳ ✳

10 ways things would be different if Bill Gates had run Enron:

10. No one would have to ask, "Who's in charge?"

9. "Creative" and "Accounting" would never be found in the same sentence.

8. Offshore partnerships would have profits, not funny names.

7. Financial reports would not appear among *NY Times* fiction best sellers.

6. Board of Directors would not be contemplating mass suicide.

5. "Dupe" would only apply to CD production, not management style.

4. Employee shareholders would be updating portfolios not resumes.

3. Two words: real profits.

2. Congress would be investigating unfair competition, not premature death.

1. The company would still be ALIVE!!!

✳ ✳ ✳

National Missile Defense Interceptor Fails Test

Missile misses intercept, destroys Enron record storage facility

Washington, D.C. (AP) -- In a major setback for the National Missile Defense (NMD) development program today, a prototype of the Extended Range Interceptor missile launched from Johnson Island in the U.S. Pacific test range missed a dummy warhead carried by a Minuteman missile launched from Vandenberg Air Force Base in Lompoc, California.

Intended as a test of whether or not the prototype strategic defense system could differentiate between a warhead and several decoys, the interceptor was supposed to intercept the target in space over the Pacific Ocean mid-way between Vandenberg and Johnson Island. Instead, the missile missed the test warhead and made a direct hit on an Enron document archive facility in Houston, Texas.

Pentagon officials were quick to point out that a complete review of telemetry data would be required to ascertain whether or not the test would be classified as a partial success or as a partial failure.

"We don't have final data yet but right now it sort of looks like we missed the incoming warhead by about 7,600 nautical miles," said Air Force General Richard B. Meyers. "Since the test objective for the intercept was 50 yards or less we are, of course, disappointed. However, we don't want to be too hasty and jump to any conclusions. We're going to need to review all of the flight data to understand the complete results. Even though the flight path and final point of impact were somewhat unexpected, somewhere in flight the missile may have been close enough to the incoming warhead to constitute a near miss; it may not end up being as bad as it looks."

The briefing by Pentagon officials pointed out that certain aspects of the test went exactly according to plan. In particular, performance of the kinetic impact warhead appears to have met or even exceeded expectations. "Based upon the damage to the

Enron facility and surrounding area," said the General, "It appears that the warhead definitely has more than enough destructive capability to fulfill mission requirements."

The Enron secure document archive facility was disguised to look like a trailer park and housed the originals of several hundred thousand one of a kind, highly confidential Enron corporate records dating back to 1985. The facility was located in Fairbanks, Texas, a suburb northwest of Houston. A spokesman for Enron confirmed that virtually all of the records were destroyed by the missile impact, the subsequent six-alarm fire and the ensuing water damage.

Ken Lay released a personal statement saying, "Oh, darn. I hope this doesn't cause any inconvenience to the ongoing investigations."

With multiple committees in the U.S. House of Representatives and the U.S. Senate simultaneously investigating Enron, the coincidence of the missile impact on an Enron record storage facility has raised eyebrows all across Washington D.C.

"This just further increases my concerns about the proposed missile defense system," said Senate Majority Leader Tom Daschle (D-S.D.), "Not only does it appear to be unable to hit its intended targets, in this case it seems to have managed to destroy critical evidence of wrongdoing by Enron executives half a continent away. We'll be following the investigation into this highly irregular launch very closely and members of House and Senate committees may have some questions of their own."

White House Press Secretary Ari Fleischer read a prepared statement that reiterated President Bush's continued strong support for the NMD program. "I remain confident that long term the NMD program is a central part of our long term security," said the President, "And the fact that a test mishap just happened to eliminate a lot of old Enron documents does nothing to diminish my enthusiasm for the project."

Secret Enron Employee Performance Review Meanings

Review Term	Secret Meaning
Good presentation skills	Can bullshit standing up
Good communication skills	Spends lots of time on phone
Well qualified	Married to a Democrat
Exceptionally well qualified	Married to a Republican
Work is first priority	Has no life
Socially active	Drinks a lot
Family is socially active	Spouse drinks a lot, too
Works well independently	Nobody knows what they do
Works well in the field	Never shows up in the office
Highly intelligent	Wears glasses
Agile intellect	Probably has A.D.D.
Quick thinking	Always has a good excuse
Confrontational style	Punches co-workers
Very confrontational style	Punches boss
Highly focused	Does one thing at a time
Thoughtful	Sleeps at desk
Analytical	Can't make a decision
Careful	Won't make a decision
Aggressive	Obnoxious
Delegates well	Gets someone else to do work
Good command of language	Speaks English
Attentive to details	Nit picker
Highly attentive to details	Anal retentive nit picker
Good leadership qualities	Intimidates others
Good judgement	Flips coin to makes decision
Exceptionally good judgment	Agrees with boss's decisions
Team player	Ass kisser
Strong team player	Exceptionally good ass kisser
Good sense of humor	Laughs at bosses jokes
Career minded	Back stabber
Loyal	Not subpoenaed yet

✶ ✶ ✶

An Arthur Andersen auditor, an Enron accountant and Enron CFO Andrew Fastow were on their way back to the Enron headquarters in Houston when they were all killed in a car wreck. Upon arriving outside the Pearly Gates they are surprised to find themselves waiting in line with Alan Greenspan who had died suddenly that same day. It looked like it was going to be a long wait in line, so to pass the time, Greenspan asked them to each tell him a little bit about themselves.

The Arthur Andersen auditor replied first that he had an MBA from Harvard, he had over 15 years of CPA experience at Andersen and his IQ was 160.

"Wonderful," said Greenspan, "We can discuss monetary policy and its effect on the growth of the economy." Turning to the Enron accountant, Greenspan asked, "How about you?"

The accountant replied that he was a Rice University graduate, with a BA in accounting, he'd worked at Enron for 5 years and his IQ was 135.

"Fine," said Greenspan, "We can discuss the impact proposed GAAP changes could have on corporate expense reporting and revenue recognition." Finally, he turned to Fastow and asked, "What about you?"

Fastow replied that he had an MBA from Northwestern, he'd been the CFO of Enron since 1998 but he didn't know his IQ.

"So," replied Greenspan after some thought, "How about those Astros?"

Not long ago Enron was poised on the edge of the abyss. Since then they have taken great strides forward.

We have been unable to confirm the rumor that the U.S. House of Representatives and the Senate delayed the start of their various investigations into the Enron scandal until they had confirmed that all money budgeted by Enron for political contributions prior to their bankruptcy filing had, in fact, been distributed to all of the intended recipients.

✳ ✳ ✳

Dear Abby:

I am facing a very serious problem and I need your advice. I am engaged to the most beautiful, sweetest girl in the world. She is seventeen and we plan marry as soon as she turns eighteen. My problem is that I am concerned that her family and mine may not get along. I am a Vietnam-era deserter from the Army. My mother runs a pro-Nazi information site on the Internet and my father (a former dentist) is in prison doing 25 to life for molesting female patients while they were under anesthesia.

The primary support for our family comes from my sales of phony credit cards, my uncle (master pickpocket Nicky "The Hand" Moreno), my twin kid sisters (well known for their "twins" 900 number: 900-2FORYOU and XXX website: www.ucando2.com) and my cousin who works in accounting at Enron.

Her family, by contrast, seems pretty normal so I am naturally worried that my family may not make a good impression on hers. We are all scheduled to get acquainted at dinner next week. In your opinion, should I or shouldn't I, tell her about my cousin who works for Enron?

Yours,

"Nervous"

Dear Nervous,

Yes, it looks like you have a real problem. The good news is that barring early parole it looks unlikely that your father will end up attending the dinner. I suggest you say that you work in "credit management" and then introduce your mother as an "Internet entrepreneur", uncle as "an independent businessman" and your sisters as "online content providers". That just leaves your cousin who works at Enron. If your bride to be and her family seem open minded (and none of them lost money on Enron stock!) you can probably risk telling them the truth. Otherwise, you might just say that your cousin is a "creative writer".

Good luck.

Abby

✳ ✳ ✳

After a few drinks at Rudyard's in Houston a little guy leans over to the big guy next to him at the bar and says, "Want to hear the latest Enron joke?"

The big guy glares at him and replies, "Well, friend, before you tell that joke you should know that I'm 6'1", 210 pounds, a former Marine and before the collapse I was an Enron accountant."

Before the guy with the joke can say anything back, the even bigger guy next to the big guy says, "I'm 6'3", 230 pounds, a former Green Beret and before the collapse I, too, was an Enron accountant."

Finally, the huge guy down the bar next to the bigger guy says, "I'm 6'5", 260 pounds, a former SEAL and before the collapse I, too, was an Enron accountant."

The big guy now turns back to the joker (who is all of 5'8", 165 pounds soaking wet) and says, "Now, friend, do you still want to tell that Enron joke?"

"No, I guess not," the little joker replies, "I'd really hate to have to explain it three times."

Enron May Buy Itself Out Of Bankruptcy

Stock hedge strategy could pay off for Houston energy giant

Houston, TX (AP) -- In yet another bizarre twist to the Enron bankruptcy saga it was today learned that Enron may be in a position to buy itself out of bankruptcy. A court ordered review of assets has revealed that one of Enron's many offshore partnerships which had been speculating in Enron stock when the stock plummeted has holdings that now appear to be worth several hundred billion dollars – more than enough to allow Houston based Enron to resume operations.

The Bermuda based offshore partnership, "Chewy, Chewy, Cocoa Puffs Partners IV, LTD", was hedging using a variation on the obscure, highly technical Black-Scholes derivative double inverted crawfish straddle with a half twist. When the share price of Enron stock plunged the value of the partnership's derivative positions skyrocketed. Assuming all the positions are liquidated, bankrupt Enron could find itself in the unique position of being owned by an offshore partnership with billions in assets that it in turn owns.

"It could take a while to sort out who owns what," conceded Federal Bankruptcy Court Judge Arthur J. Gonzales, "It's sort of like one of those Mobius strips - it makes my head hurt to just think about it."

There were unconfirmed rumors that the Enron Board of Directors was preparing to immediately re-instate Ken Lay and the rest of the Enron management team. One source close to the situation who spoke on condition of anonymity summed up the Enron Board's position: "Hey, it looks like all those offshore partnerships might not have been such a bad idea after all. Who cares if nobody understood them - talk about snatching victory from the jaws of defeat!! It looks like some heavy duty management bonuses are definitely going to be in order here. The real question is should we hire back any of the employees and resume operations or just distribute the cash and go have fun?"

✱ ✱ ✱

10 New Year's Resolutions Enron should have made years earlier:

For next year we will...

10.   Learn to add.

9.   Leave cute *Star Wars* names for moviemakers and toy builders.

8.   Trim our hedges.

7.   Limit use of "offshore" to energy exploration.

6.   Eschew obfuscation.

5.   Understand our own business model.

4.   Count more on performance, less on politicians.

3.   Two words: real profits.

2.   Keep the CEO in the loop.

1.   Keep the other nine resolutions past January 2.

With all the wealth created by Enron's rise, some Enron executives became a bit materialistic. A finance executive and an exploration vice president were comparing the features of their huge new sport utility vehicles.

"Nice SUV," said the finance guy. "Fully loaded?"

"Yes, I think so."

"I've got a two channel cell phone with fax and wireless remote Internet hookup," pointed out the marketer, looking for a feature his friend might have missed.

"Me, too."

"Got a television?"

"Of course," replied the exploration VP, getting into the spirit of the game. "I've got a full home theater setup with sixteen speakers."

"Got a bed?" asked the finance exec.

"Uh, No. You've got a bed??"

"Yeah, I had to have it put in custom but it's a really cool feature," replied the finance guy, thrilled to have found something that he had and his friend didn't. "Now when I work late I can crash right here and I don't have to drive home."

Really put out at being 'out featured', the exploration VP went back to the SUV dealer and demanded that a custom bed be installed.

A couple weeks later, working late as usual, the developer noticed the marketing executive's vehicle in the parking lot. The lights were on and he could hear the stereo playing. Unable to resist, he stopped and knocked on the window. No response. He knocked louder. No response. Anxious to show that he had caught up in the feature race, he pounded on the door. Finally, the finance guy rolled down the window and asked, "What do you want?"

"Hi," began the exploration VP. "I just wanted to tell you that now I've got a bed in my SUV, too, and mine has deep heat and a built in variable speed massager."

"Do you mean to tell me that you got me out of the hot tub just to tell me that?"

✻ ✻ ✻

Enron Business Haikus

Business model
Too complex to understand.
It's a house of cards.

Buy low and sell high.
Our intermediations
Raise energy costs.

Our profits are made
At the consumer's expense.
Pass the caviar.

Stock price fell today.
Management says, 'Don't fear'
I am still afraid.

Chaos reigns within.
Reflect, repent and sell short.
Even down can be up.

✻ ✻ ✻

10 Things Enron will never admit in public:

10. Tried to corner market on bovine methane.

9. Originally wanted to name the Astro's stadium, "Enron Has You By The Balls Field".

8. Secretly worked with auto manufacturers to decrease SUV gas mileage.

7. Tried to get Kyoto treaty renamed and moved to Houston.

6. Secretly gave 200,000 electric air conditioners to California residents at the height of the energy crisis.

5. Rejected secret recommendation from Accenture that they fire Arthur Andersen accounting.

4. Rejected REALLY secret recommendation from Arthur Andersen accounting that they fire Accenture.

3. Rejected REALLY, REALLY secret recommendation from Arthur Andersen accounting that they fire Arthur Andersen accounting.

2. More executive members of the "mile high club" than any Fortune 500 company.

1. <u>Nobody</u> understood the business model.

Competition for the very top jobs at Enron was really tough. To make it to the top you had to demonstrate talent, ability, aggressiveness, a bad memory and, perhaps most important, total, unswerving loyalty to Enron. For one particularly plum assignment the selection process had narrowed down to three candidates. All had been with Enron for some time and all had impeccable credentials. Each was to be given a two-hour stress interview designed by Accenture to select the best possible candidate. As part of the final interview process each had been requested to bring their spouse along to the interview at the headquarters in Houston.

With his wife waiting in the lobby, the first candidate went in for his stress interview. At the end of the interview, one of the interviewers began his summary: "You are a great candidate. As one final test of your total loyalty to Enron take this gun, go into the lobby, shoot your wife and the job will be yours."

Taken aback, the candidate jumped to his feet, shouted, "You must be out of your mind! I love my wife madly. We have two small children. I could never hurt her. TAKE THIS JOB AND SHOVE IT!!" and sprinted out the door never to be seen again.

The second candidate arrived and went in for her interview. At the end of the interview, the lead interviewer gave the same summary: "You are a great candidate. As one final test of your total loyalty to Enron take this gun, go into the lobby, shoot your husband and the job will be yours."

Thinking about it for several minutes, the candidate finally replied, "I know the job requires a lot of loyalty and I can see how you would use a pressure situation like this to test it, but I really don't think I can do it. My husband and I have been together for many years, we're very comfortable together and the promotion is just not worth it to me. I'll just stay where I am. Please withdraw my name from further consideration." She then got up and left to return to her office.

The third candidate arrived and went in for his interview. As before, at the end of the interview the lead interviewer gave his summary: "You are a great candidate. As one final test of your total loyalty to Enron take this gun, go into the lobby, shoot your wife and the job is yours."

Without hesitation the candidate got up, took the gun and headed back to the lobby.

BANG. . . . . .BANG, BANG, BANG, BANG, BANG.

THUMP. . . . . .THUMP, THUMP, THUMP, THUMP.

Upon re-entering the interview room, the confused interviewer asked the disheveled and out of breath candidate, "What the hell was all that **THUMPING?**"

"Oh, that," responded the candidate while calmly combing his hair and straightening his clothes, "Some moron put blanks in the gun. Scared her good, but I had to finish her off with a lobby chair."

✳ ✳ ✳

Back before the collapse, Enron Chairman Ken Lay and former CEO Jeffrey Skilling were at a management planning session at Lay's Aspen condo. During a break one afternoon they were out hiking in the woods when they found their path blocked by a huge grizzly bear. They reversed course immediately but were dismayed to find that the bear was following them and looking most unfriendly. Skilling quickly stopped, took off his daypack, removed his mountain hiking boots and started to put on his running shoes.

"Jeff," said Lay, "This is stupid. Forget it. You can't possibly outrun a grizzly bear."

"Ken," said Skilling, "I don't have to outrun the bear. I just have to outrun you."

✳ ✳ ✳

Q. How do you know when an Enron executive has started lying during his Congressional testimony?

A. When his lips have started moving.

✱ ✱ ✱

Enron exploration operations in Alaska were not always pleasant places to be in the dead of winter. One bitter afternoon as the winds howled, the snow drifted and the temperature dropped toward –60F, an electrician at an Enron construction project near the Alaska pipeline noticed an ironworker stop what he was doing, climb down off the structure and walk away.

"Where are you going?" the electrician called out.

"To get some warmer clothes."

"Where are they?"

"In San Diego," yelled the ironworker as he climbed into his land cruiser and sped off.

✱ ✱ ✱

Even laid end to end all of the executives, accountants, lawyers and consultants at Enron still couldn't make ends meet.

✱ ✱ ✱

Q. What did they do to the Enron engineer who started to take Viagra?

A. Sent him into the oil fields as a drill rig erector.

✱ ✱ ✱

Enron executive perspective on testifying before Congress:

Better to remain silent and appear a dupe than to open your mouth and remove all doubt.

✱ ✱ ✱

The following email was received at the Enron Human Resource center:

Date: Mon, 08 Oct 2001 13:10:03 -0600
To: personnelreviews@enron.hr.com
From: amanager@enron.explore.com
RE: Performance review for Nathan H.

While working as Nathan's supervisor, I usually find him working studiously and efficiently in field exploration without gossiping with other workers in the department. He never spends time on useless tasks. When assigned work, he always finishes his assignments on time. A loner, Nathan is most often working in the field engrossed in projects and he is never found wasting time around the office. He has absolutely no problems with his peers despite his high levels of skill and deep knowledge of this technical field. I strongly feel he should be promoted and in the event of any downsizing he should not be terminated or reassigned.

Not long thereafter, a second email arrived:

Date: Mon, 08 Oct 2001 13:52:03 -0600
To: personnelreviews@enron.hr.com
From: amanager@enron.explore.com
RE: Earlier email performance review for Nathan H....

Nathan was in my office looking at my computer screen when I was typing the performance review sent to you earlier today. For my true assessment of this cretin read only every other line - i.e. 1, 3, 5, 7...

* * *

During the boom times Enron spent a great deal of time and money sending representatives to college campuses to recruit the best young engineering and business talent. Reaching the end of a job interview, one recruiter asked a particularly promising young MBA due to graduate from Stanford, "What sort of starting salary were you thinking about?"

After thinking a few moments the fledgling business tycoon replied, "In the neighborhood of $150,000 a year, depending on the benefits package."

The recruiter said, "Well, what would you say to a package with $150,000 base salary, quarterly bonuses, five weeks vacation, twelve paid holidays, full medical, dental, vision, life and disability insurance, an Enron 401(K) retirement fund where we match up to 100% of your annual contribution, generous stock options and a new leased company car every two years - say, a Porsche Boxster S?"

The young MBA, thinking she had hit the mother lode, sat up straight and said, "Wow! Are you kidding?"

"Yeah", the recruiter replied, "But you started it."

✷ ✷ ✷

An Enron security guard had been missing from work for over a week when someone finally noticed that he was missing. After several calls to his home went unreturned his supervisor became concerned and called the police. When they arrived at his apartment and pounded on the door there was no answer so they broke through the door but alas found him dead in the shower, water still running, an empty bottle of organic shampoo next to his shriveled body.

What had happened? Was it foul play? Natural causes? Suicide? Who was to blame? The mystery was finally solved, when one of his fellow security guards picked up the shampoo bottle and read the instructions:

> Wet hair
> Apply shampoo to hair
> Lather
> Rinse hair thoroughly
> Repeat

10 New possible spokespeople for Enron:

10. **Rodney Dangerfield**

9. **Joe Bfstplk**

8. **Cassandra**

7. **Harold Hill**

6. **Jack Kevorkian**

5. **Al Capone**

4. **Harcord Fenton Mudd**

3. **Henry Gondorf**

2. **Charles K. Ponzi**

1. **Thomas Crown**

God, having reached the end of His patience with the human race, decides to send down His angels to destroy the earth. Wanting to give the people at least some opportunity to repent, He summons the Pope, George W. Bush and Ken Lay and informs them that the world will end at precisely 12:01 AM, GMT, two weeks from this day of notice. Just as the three begin to leave God motions to Ken Lay to come closer and whispers something in his ear. After listening, Lay nods his head in understanding and then leaves to catch up with the others.

The Pope immediately returns to the Vatican and summons the College of Cardinals. "Well," says the Pope, "I've got some good news and some bad news. The good news is that we were right all along and there is, in fact, a God. The bad news is that He is really pissed off and the world is going to end at 12:01 AM, GMT, two weeks from today. Notify the faithful to repent and prepare."

George W. Bush immediately returns to Washington D.C. and summons his cabinet. "Well," says W., "I've got some bad news and some good news. The bad news is that God is really pissed off and He is going to destroy the world at 12:01 AM, GMT, two weeks from today. The good news is that we won't have to finish hunting down Osama bin Laden and all of those al-Qaeda terrorists. Tell Dick he can come out of the shelter."

Ken Lay immediately returns to Houston, calls up all of the pre-collapse Enron directors and executive officers and asks them to come to a special meeting. "Well," says Ken to the assembled ex-execs, "I've got some good news, some really good news and some really bad news. The good news is that even with all of Enron's problems and recent management changes God still knows exactly who we all are. The really good news is that we're not going to have to worry about finishing all of these stupid congressional hearings. The really bad news is that God told me personally that **WE'RE ALL GOING TO HELL.....**"

3.0   Investors and Investments

Q.   How did you make a small fortune in Enron stock?

A.   Start with a large one!!

A little girl asked her father, "Daddy, do all fairy tales begin with, 'Once upon a time'?"

"No Sweetie," replied Dad. "A lot of fairy tales begin with, 'Dear fellow Enron shareholders...'."

Stock Market Investment Commercial

They started with a better idea about how to sell energy. Armed with a war chest of just a few hundred million dollars, they forged ahead and took on the competition. They bought, merged, leveraged and hedged. Their financial model was so complex that no one could explain it but everyone figured it must work since earnings were good and analyst after analyst recommended the stock. Year by year their stock rose and rose until it reached an all time high of $90.56 per share.

Then someone mentioned that maybe their business model might not be so good after all. Rumors of unreported losses and questionable offshore investments surfaced. Government regulators began to ask questions. Overnight all the analysts changed their opinions from "accumulate" to "sell now". The stock plunged, the management team bailed out and the company filed for Chapter 11 bankruptcy; the stock now trades for under $1 and billions of dollars of shareholder value has been erased.

Where can you find such opportunities? Of course. NYSE - the stock market for your last $100.

Enronisms - 10 Statements from the Enron 2000 Annual Report they wish they had back (these are real!!):

10. "We are positioned to dramatically increase our profitability in FY2001." – page 16

9. "Enron is laser-focused on earnings per share and we expect to continue strong earnings performance." – page 4

8. "We have a proven business concept that is eminently scalable..." – page 7

7. "Enron's ability to deliver is the one constant in an increasingly complex and competitive world." – page 8

6. "Our people also make a difference. We are able to attract the best and the brightest and place them in an entrepreneurial atmosphere in which they can thrive." – page 11

5. "We have an obligation to communicate." – page 55

4. "We treat others as we would like to be treated ourselves." – page 55

3. "We are satisfied with nothing less than the very best in everything we do." – page 55

2. "These abilities make Enron the right company with the right model at the right time." – page 4

1. "We plan to leverage all of these competitive advantages to create significant value for our shareholders." – page 7

✱ ✱ ✱

Shareholder Haikus from Enron's Last Days

CNN today
Says Enron distress increased.
This is not good news.

Dynegy retreat
Leaves few options available.
My foreboding grows.

The merger now dead.
Hope fades to a mere glimmer.
Chapter 11 looms.

The official news
Now has tolled. Enron is gone.
So is my money.

✻ ✻ ✻

A grade school teacher in Houston was asking students what their parents did for a living. "Mikey, you go first," said the teacher.

Little Mikey stood up and proudly said, "My father is a doctor at the Rice University medical center."

"That's wonderful, Mikey. How about your father, Mary?"

Mary stood up and shyly said, "My father is a Houston fireman."

"Thank you, Mary. What does your father do, Billy?"

Billy proudly stood up and announced, "My daddy plays piano in a Galveston whorehouse."

The teacher was shocked and went to Billy's house. When Billy's father came to the door the teacher repeated what his son had said in class and demanded the father explain. Billy's dad said, "I just use the piano player thing as a cover. I actually work in shareholder relations at Enron. These days, how can I explain a job like that to a six year old child?"

✻ ✻ ✻

ENRON ANNUAL REPORT LANGUAGE DECODER

What They Say	What It Means
COMPLEX BUSINESS MODEL	Even the CPA firm doesn't have a clue what we really do.
SCALABLE	We think we can sell more than one.
BUSINESS UNIT	Separate company within a company. Corporate feudalism at work.
CONSOLIDATE	Mix the results from the good and bad business units together so you can't tell what is what.
AMORTIZE	Spread the really expensive bad news out over several years.
ONE TIME CHARGE	Something so stupid that we can't amortize it.
PRO-FORMA	What the results look like with reality removed.
RE-STATE	Convert reality to pro-forma by removing consolidation costs, amortization, one time charges, etc.
OFFSHORE PARTNERSHIP	Convenient place to hide stuff we don't want to re-state right now.

What They Say	What It Means
OFF BALANCE SHEET	Where the liabilities from all of the offshore partnerships tend to turn up. (see "Contingent Liability".)
CONTINGENT LIABILITY	Something stupid we won't end up paying for if we're real lucky. (Otherwise, see "One Time Charge".)
HEDGE	Bet things will go up and down at the same time.
LEVERAGE	Borrow against stuff we don't own to buy stuff we can't afford.
COMMUNITY SERVICE	What a lot of our executives are going to be doing after their trials.
YEARS IN DEVELOPMENT	We've been pissing your money down this rat hole for a long time.
INCENTIVE COMPENSATION	Our executive's version of "pay yourself first."
GAAP COMPLIANT	Our accountants may be able to explain some of this bullshit but we can't.
SHAREHOLDER VALUE	Having someone to sell the stock to when the management sells out.

✳ ✳ ✳

10 Lines from Enron shareholder relations that told you there were BIG problems:

10. "Was early retirement a *real* priority for you?"

9. "My lawyer wouldn't want me to answer that question."

8. "Have you considered calling '911'?"

7. "I'm sorry but we've been instructed to play dumb."

6. "Have you ever heard of 'cost averaging'?"

5. "Think of all the profits from other stocks you'll be able to offset."

4. "When did you say your child starts college?"

3. "I'll call you back later if I find out anything."

2. "You <u>DO</u> have a diversified portfolio, don't you?"

1. "Uhhh ... I sold all my shares last month."

A guy walking along the beach on South Padre Island finds a bottle floating in the surf and picks it up. When he pulls out the cork there is a bright flash, a puff of blue smoke and a genie pops out and says, "Thank you for releasing me. For your kindness, I will grant you one wish."

The guy says, "I've always wanted to visit Hawaii, but I can't because I'm afraid to fly and I get deathly seasick on ships. So my wish is for you to build a bridge from San Diego to Honolulu so that I can drive to Hawaii in my car."

The genie says, "I'm sorry, but I just don't think I can do that. The amount of work involved is unimaginable. Just think of all the cement and steel that would be needed to build the huge pilings and abutments required to hold up the bridge – they would need to reach thousands of feet down to the bottom of the Pacific Ocean. Plus, since the bridge would be over 2,200 miles long, there would have to be gas stations, restaurants and rest stops all along the way. No, that is just too much to ask. You're just going to have to come up with another wish."

Disappointed, the guy thinks for a couple minutes then says, "Well, there is one other thing. I lost a lot of money when Enron went belly up and I've been baffled by the whole Enron scandal. I'd really like to understand their business model. How did they accelerate revenue recognition? How did they hide liabilities offshore? How did their individual business units work? How did they do all those wildly irregular partnership transactions right under the nose of one of the largest CPA firms in the world and still not get caught? Why did it take so long for the SEC and other regulators to catch up with them? I want to know everything that made Enron tick! Explain it to me!!"

The genie thinks for a second then says, "OK, fine. So would that bridge to Hawaii be two lanes or four?"

10 Ways to recycle old Enron stock certificates:

10. Origami pig and other farm animals.

9. Paper airplanes.

8. Fireplace starter.

7. Shred for confetti.

6. Laminate for place mats.

5. Cut into 4" x 4" squares. Decoupage onto cork squares for drink coasters.

4. Gift wrap for small packages.

3. Frame and hang on wall as reminder.

2. Shred into strips. Braid into rope. Hang yourself.

1. Very swanky birdcage liner

Before the collapse, Enron spent considerable time and effort making sure Wall Street held the company in high esteem. CFO Andrew Fastow would routinely travel to New York to brief investment bankers and industry analysts regarding ongoing Enron financial performance. On one visit he was asked, "How did your meeting with the analysts go?" by Neil Cavuto on Fox News Network.

"Just fine," replied the satisfied Fastow, "We had a very good discussion and a frank exchange of views. The analysts came in with their views and they left with ours."

The crash of Enron has disrupted the financial plans of thousands of families across the country. One couple who had been getting significant investment income from the dividends on their Enron stock sat down to go over their household budget to see what expense cuts they would need to make to balance the budget without the dividend income.

"My dear," the husband said to his wife, "If you'd just learn to get around better in the kitchen we could fire the cook."

"My dear," retorted his wife, "If you'd just learn to get around better in the bedroom we could fire the gardener."

Q. What are three differences between a hard on and an Enron?

A1. A hard on can only screw one shareholder at a time.

A2. If a hard on goes down you can usually get it back up again.

A3. It's very difficult to fake the performance of a hard on.

10 Least Popular Enron Offshore Partnerships:

10. Indonesian Compost Compactors, LLP

9. North Sea Seal Mulch, Ltd

8. Russian Plutonium Reprocessors, LLC

7. Pinatubo Natural Gas, LLC

6. Cal-Mex Burrito Gas Holdings, LP

5. Chernobyl Energy Explorations, Ltd

4. Costa Rican Guano Partners IV

3. Argentine Bloated Cow Resources, Ltd

2. Mexican Chicken Methane, LLP

1. Shanghai Human Dung Consolidators, LLC

✳ ✳ ✳

4.0   Executives and Consultants

Q.   How many Enron executives does it take to change a light bulb?

A.   None. They anticipate when the bulb will burn out, sell off their stock and then bail out before it gets too dark.

✱ ✱ ✱

A young Enron manager was leaving the office late one evening when he found CEO Ken Lay standing in front of a paper shredder with a piece of paper in his hand. "Listen," said the CEO, "This is a very sensitive and important document and my secretary has gone for the night. Can you make this thing work?"

"Certainly," said the young executive. He turned the machine on, inserted the paper, and pressed the start button.

"Excellent, excellent!" said the CEO as his paper disappeared inside the machine. "I only need one copy!"

✱ ✱ ✱

Q.   How do you keep an Enron executive from drowning?

A.   Shoot him before he hits the water.

✱ ✱ ✱

Sign on the wall of an Enron Executive's office:

If the ends don't justify the means:

You're doing the math wrong!!

✱ ✱ ✱

GUIDE TO ENRON MANAGEMENT MEMO TERMS AND EXPRESSIONS

What They Say	What It Means
I'm looking at a number of different approaches.	I have no clue what to do at this point.
Close project coordination.	Let's get together for lunch.
We're forming a consensus.	Nobody agrees with me on this.
Let's compare notes.	Maybe I can steal an idea from you.
We need to flesh this out more.	Not enough bullshit yet.
I have to push back on that.	Probably the dumbest idea I've ever heard.
I'm having an extensive report prepared on a fresh approach.	I just hired three new MBAs who have no clue what to do.
The entire concept had to be abandoned.	Even I couldn't get this one past the auditors.
It is "in process".	Major internal politics involved; there is no chance it will ever happen.
I will look into it.	Forget it! I already have too many problems.
Please keep me in the loop.	It's your baby, now!

What They Say	What It Means
Please note and initial.	I'm spreading the responsibility for this.
Give me your interpretation.	I can't wait to hear your bullshit.
We need input from the top.	No way am I taking the hit for this turkey.
We need input from the staff.	They feel better when they think I listened to them.
Give me the benefit of your thinking.	I'll listen as long as what you say doesn't interfere with what I've already done or what I plan to do.
Let's schedule a conference call for the team.	I could use a nap.
Let's discuss in person.	I screwed up.
See me.	Come to my office, I really screwed up.
I'm following our standards.	That's the way I have always done it.
e-mail me the data.	I'm too lazy to write it down.
I didn't get your e-mail.	I didn't look. I haven't checked my e-mail for days.

✳ ✳ ✳

An Enron executive became severely depressed after the company's sudden collapse. His wife went to the doctor to get help in reviving her man's sex drive. "What about trying Viagra?" asked the doctor.

"No way," replied the distraught wife. "I can't even get him to take an aspirin for his constant headaches."

"No problem. Grind the pill up and put the powder into his coffee; he won't even taste it. Try it and come back in a week to let me know how it worked."

A week later the wife returned and the doctor inquired as to the results. "Oh, it was horrible, just horrible, doctor," cried the wife, bursting into tears.

"What happened?"

"Well, I did just as you advised," she replied. "I ground up the pill and slipped the powder into his coffee. After about ten minutes the effect was amazing. He jumped up from the chair, swept everything off the table, ripped my clothes off and then proceeded to make mad, passionate love to me right there on the tabletop. It was terrible!!"

"What was so terrible about that? I thought you wanted a more exciting sex life."

"Oh, no doctor, please don't misunderstand! The sex was the best we've had in 15 years, but I'll never be able to show my face at that restaurant again."

✳ ✳ ✳

Q. What's the best thing to throw to a drowning Enron executive?

A. An anvil.

Q. What's the definition of *ambivalence*?

A. An Enron executive driving off a cliff in your new Ferrari.

✳ ✳ ✳

One of the heaviest elements known to science is Enronium. This amazing element has no neutrons, protons or electrons. Instead, it has a nucleus composed of one enron (a recently discovered particle that is amazingly dense and uncharged - at least as of this date), two executive vice-enrons, ten senior vice-enrons, 18 vice-enrons, and 36 assistant vice-enrons.

The Enronium nucleus is surrounded by a thick shell composed of a huge number of another recently discovered particle, the "moron". Morons travel around the nucleus in circles, ellipses, squares and pretty much any other random shaped orbit they feel like.

Enronium is highly inert and does not decay. Instead, it institutes a continuing series of reviews and reorganizations, which continuously shuffle the positions of all particles. This guarantees that none of the particles really know what is going on throughout the rest of the atom. Atoms of Enronium spontaneously form into molecules known as "Business Units" by exchanging packets of "memos" (another recently discovered particle) with each other.

✳ ✳ ✳

Q. What do you call 25 skydiving Enron executives falling through the sky?

A. Skeet

✳ ✳ ✳

Before the Enron collapse, then CEO Jeffrey Skilling made a proposal to the Vatican: Enron would make a $1 billion donation to the Catholic Church in return for one small change to the Bible. He insisted, however, that he would only discuss the proposal in detail with the Pope himself. The Curia was pretty sure that this was not going to be a good deal but since a billion dollars would have been useful to the Church's work an audience was arranged. Shortly after it began the sound of muffled shouting was heard from the Pope's chambers. The door flew open and Skilling stomped out of the room.

"What did he propose, your Holiness," the curious cardinals asked the obviously irritated Pope.

"Oh, not much," huffed the pissed off Pontiff. "Just that we replace 'Amen' with 'Enron'!!"

✳ ✳ ✳

Q.   Why do they bury Enron senior executives at least 20 feet under ground?

A.   Deep down they are really good people.

✳ ✳ ✳

In school one day the teacher asked the students if anyone could give him an example of a "tragedy". Little Billy stood up and said, "If my best friend was playing in the street and a car came along and killed him, would that be a tragedy?"

"No," the teacher said, "That would be an 'accident'."

Annie then raised her hand, "If a school bus carrying fifty children drove off a cliff, killing them all, would that be a tragedy?"

"I'm afraid not," explained the teacher. "While very sad, that is what we would call a 'great loss'."

The room is silent; no more students volunteer.

"What?" Asked the teacher, "Isn't there anyone in class who can give me an example of a tragedy?"

Finally, little Jackie in the back of the room raised his hand. He stood up and in a timid voice said, "If a corporate jet carrying a lot of the members of the Enron executive staff was blown up in mid-air by a terrorist bomb, would that be a tragedy?"

"That's a very good example, Jackie!" The teacher exclaimed. "Now can you tell me why it's a tragedy?"

"Well," said little Jackie, "It wouldn't be an accident, and it certainly would be no great loss!"

✳ ✳ ✳

When things were still booming for Enron, CEO Jeffrey Skilling, back in New York for one of his regular meetings with stock market analysts, was in the elevator on the way to his room. After the other passengers got off, he found himself alone with a lovely young blonde dressed in a tight fitting, low cut red cocktail dress that left very little to the imagination.

"Mr. Skilling," she said breathlessly, leaning in so he could smell her intoxicating perfume, "I work for ConED. I recognize you from the *Wall Street Journal*. I think you and Enron are just so amazing. You're so rich and so powerful and so sexy that I just want to stop the elevator and make love to you right here, right now."

"So," said Skilling, "What's in it for me?"

✳ ✳ ✳

Q.   How many Accenture consultants does it take to change a light bulb?

A.   That's difficult to say. First, we initiate a study to see if light is even needed in the area. Then we determine why the bulb burned out and perform an analysis to verify it's the right type of bulb. At that point we could be go/no-go to initiate a bulb change action - although we may recommend some additional studies to determine the light requirements of all classes of users who visit that area. Once a bulb change action has been initiated we can develop RFQs, evaluate the qualifications of possible bulb changers to perform the task at zero defects, recommend personnel, supervise the change and perform post-change light quality monitoring.

✳ ✳ ✳

10 Exciting New Career Opportunities For Former Enron Executives:

10. Ejector seat maintenance

9. Used commodity future sales

8. Psychic hotline operator

7. Professional cheese shredder

6. Teach creative obfuscation

5. Casino operator

4. Sky diving instructor

3. Commentator on Felony News Network

2. Arthur Andersen auditor

1. Three words: professional document disposal

Not to mention...

The many exciting opportunities in mandatory community service that many of them are likely to be offered...

✳ ✳ ✳

Enron Managers

(Parody lyrics sung to melody of "Mrs. Robinson", by Paul Simon)

And here's to you Enron managers.
Cheney loves you more than you will know.
Whoa! Whoa! Whoa!

God bless you please Enron managers.
Money's gone so now you have to pay!
Pay! Pay! Pay!
Pay! Pay! Pay!

We'd like to have
More details how you spent it
For our files.
We'd like to have you tell us
Who you paid.
Look around you. All you see
Are press and TV guys.
Take the fifth unless
You want to go to jail.

And here's to you, Enron managers.
Cheney loves you more than you will know.
Whoa! Whoa! Whoa!

God bless you, please, Enron managers.
Money's gone so now you have to pay!
Pay! Pay! Pay!
Pay! Pay! Pay!

Hide it in a Cayman bank
Where no one ever goes.
Pay it to the Congress for your projects.
It's a little secret,
Just an Enron board affair.
Most of all you've got to hide it
From the press.

Coo Coo ca choo, Enron Managers.
Cheney loves you more than you will know.
Whoa! Whoa! Whoa!

God bless you, please, Enron managers.
Money's gone so now you have to pay!
Pay! Pay! Pay!
Pay! Pay! Pay!

Sitting on a slush fund
Full of cash and other perks.
Paying it to candidates in crates.
Democrats,
Republicans,
There's no need to choose.
When the votes take place you never lose.

Where have you gone, Kenny Lay and friends?
The shareholders are looking now for you.
Woo! Woo! Woo!

What's that you say, Enron managers?
"Kenny Boy has bailed and gone away."
Hey! Hey! Hey!
Hey! Hey! Hey!

✳ ✳ ✳

One day in the autumn of 2001, the minister saw Matthew, an Enron Senior VP, walking slowly out of the church after Sunday services. From his disheveled appearance it was clear that Matthew was depressed and dejected – he looked really bad.

"Matthew," asked the concerned minister, "You look terrible. What is the matter?"

"I really can't talk about it, pastor," replied the depressed Matthew.

"Come on," coaxed the minister. "It can't be all that bad."

"Well, you have to promise to keep this completely confidential," replied Matthew. "Nobody knows it yet but Enron is in really big trouble. Our offshore partnerships are turning out to be disasters, energy prices are down, our Internet investments are tanking, our operating costs are up. I just don't know what the company is going to do."

"Matthew, every business has to face challenges from time to time; it's all part of business. Have faith. I suggest you look for your answer in the Bible," the minister counseled.

Several months later the minister again saw Matthew coming out of the Church. This time, however, he was smiling, relaxed and looking much better.

"Matthew," said the minister, "You're looking much better! Did you follow my advice?"

"Yes, I did." replied Matthew. "After our talk a couple of months ago I went home that morning and made up my mind to pray for guidance. I decided I'd just open my Bible at random, look on whatever page it opened to and then follow the first advice I saw. So, I prayed, 'Please God, give me guidance' and when I opened the Bible and looked down at the page the first phrase I saw said:

Matthew: Chapter 11."

✳ ✳ ✳

A man in a Houston antique shop noticed a large sculpture on the back of one shelf. Reaching back, he found that it was a large, wonderfully detailed brass casting of a rat. "What a great paper weight," he thought to himself. After haggling with the shop keeper over the price, he finally purchased the sculpture and left.

As he walked down the street, he thought he heard squeaking and scurrying noises behind him. He looked around and was astounded to see hoards of rats pouring out of the streets and alleys and heading straight for him. In a panic he ran down the street with a giant pack of rats in hot pursuit. The street ended at the edge of Buffalo Bayou; exhausted, he ran to the end of the pavement and in desperation heaved the brass rat as far out into the water as he could. Amazingly, the rats scurried around him and leapt into the water where they all drowned. After breathing a huge sigh of relief and resting for a few minutes, the man headed back to the curio shop.

"Do you want to buy another brass rat?" asked the shop keeper.

"Forget the brass rat. Do you have any brass Enron managers?"

The new Enron lobbyist slunk into the Congressman's office, looked furtively around and then pulled an envelope bulging with cash from his briefcase.

"Here's $50,000 in cash," he said to the Congressman. "My client really needs your support for the upcoming energy bill!"

The Congressman looked outraged. "What kind of a corrupt Congressman do you think I am?" he asked, angrily, his face contorted and turning a mottled purple.

The lobbyist sputtered, embarrassed. "I ... I heard from Ken Lay that we could 'work with you' and that we'd done it before!"

That calmed the Congressman down a little bit. "Look, son," he said, "Were I to take your money now it would be a gross ethical transgression!"

"Why? What makes it unethical now?" said the lobbyist. "It not like you haven't taken Enron's money before."

The Congressman looked puzzled for a moment then smiled. "I don't think you understand. Your opponents have already paid me very handsomely to vote the other way on this bill. If I were to take your money now it would present me with an unresolvable conflict of interest – why, I'd have to abstain!"

5.0   Accounting and Auditing

Q.   What's the difference between an Enron auditor's report from Arthur Andersen and a vivid sexual fantasy?

A.   The sexual fantasy is based upon things that you can imagine.

✳ ✳ ✳

An accountant in Houston goes into a pet shop to buy a parrot. The clerk shows him three identical looking parrots on a perch and says, "The parrot on the left costs $1,000."

"WOW!! That's one expensive parrot!! Why does it cost so much?" asks the accountant.

"Well," replies the clerk, "The shop owner told me that this is a genuine Arthur Andersen parrot who used to work on the Enron account. It knows how to prepare complex financial reports."

"How much does the middle parrot cost?" asks the accountant.

"That is another genuine Arthur Andersen parrot. It costs $2,000 because it can do everything the first one can do plus it knows how to prepare the complex financial reports required for parent company investments in offshore partnerships."

The startled accountant then asks about the third parrot, only to be told it, too, is another genuine Arthur Andersen parrot but that it costs a staggering $10,000!!! Needless to say, the accountant asks, "What can it do that's so special??"

"To be honest," replies the clerk, "The other two talk to it all the time and they call it 'Senior Partner' but no matter what I ask it, it just sits there and says, 'I refuse to answer that question on the grounds that the answer may tend to incriminate me'."

✳ ✳ ✳

To liven up their working relationship the Enron accounting department and their Arthur Andersen auditors decided to have a boat race on Clear lake just outside of Houston. Agreeing on a 2,000 meter course using eight man racing sculls, both teams practiced hard and by race day they were as ready as they could be. Unfortunately, to the chagrin of the Arthur Andersen team, the Enron accountants won by a solid 200 meters.

Afterwards, the Andersen audit team was very depressed and they decided that the reason for their crushing defeat had to be found. After much discussion, they called in Accenture and a work group from strategy, account management, project management and finance was set up to investigate and report back. Centers for excellence were mobilized. No expense was spared. After three months of research and investigation the work group came up with the answer and the coordinator gave the summary presentation to the assembled Arthur Andersen senior managers.

"To be brief," he said, "The problem was that Enron had eight people rowing and one person steering. We, on the other hand, had one person rowing and eight people steering."

Excited that the problem was now understood, the work group was asked to go away and come up with a plan so that Andersen could win the following year's race and assuage their damaged pride. Two months later, the work group had developed a detailed plan and the coordinator gave his short summary to the excited managers:

"Basically, the one person rowing has got to work harder."

Alas, we'll never know.

✻ ✻ ✻

It's a sunny day. You're by the pool. An Enron accountant and an Arthur Andersen auditor are both drowning and you can only save one of them. Do you go to lunch or read the paper?

✻ ✻ ✻

10 Top management excuses for the collapse of Enron:

10. "The dog ate the audit work papers so we never saw the warning signs."

9. "Don't blame me – I was out of the country visiting one of our partnerships."

8. "Bad Karma."

7. "Accidentally computed revenue in Canadian dollars."

6. "Spent too much on political contributions."

5. "Didn't spend enough on political contributions."

4. "Spent about the right amount on political contributions but spent it on the wrong politicians."

3. "California energy crisis ended sooner than we planned - uh - expected"

2. "Expected Y2K problems to cover everything up for at least one more year."

1. "Unfair competition from Microsoft (Hey, everyone else uses that, so why not us?)"

Note on the bulletin board in an Enron accounting group:

If you can understand it after one reading – it's NOT DONE.

✳ ✳ ✳

THE FIVE RULES OF ENRON ACCOUNTING

1. **DON'T THINK**

2. If you think: **DON'T SPEAK**.

3. If you think and speak: **DON'T WRITE**.

4. If you think, write and speak: **DON'T SIGN**.

5. If you think, write, speak and sign:

DON'T BE SURPRISED AT WHAT HAPPENS!!

✳ ✳ ✳

A lowly Enron staff accountant was sitting in his office late one night when the Devil appeared before him. The Devil told the accountant, "I have a proposition for you. You can have job security for the rest of your life. You will be able to prepare the most complicated financial schemes imaginable and they will withstand every audit, every investigation. The CFO will adore you and other members of the accounting staff will be in awe of you. Eventually you will rise to the top financial position in the company. The CEO will depend on you completely and you will make obscene amounts of money. All I want in exchange is your soul, your wife's soul, your children's souls and the souls of your parents, grandparents and parents-in-law."

The accountant thought about this for a moment, then asked, "So, what's the catch?"

✳ ✳ ✳

We hear that Arthur Andersen was using Enron to test out their new microwave auditors. They spend 45 minutes in your office and bill you for the whole day.

✻ ✻ ✻

What is the difference between realists, idealists and Enron auditors?

Realists, when given a difficult problem, work hard because they know that if they succeed they will be rewarded and if they fail they will be punished.

Idealists, when given a difficult problem, work hard because they believe the solution may be good for mankind and that's reward enough for them.

Enron auditors, when given a difficult problem, work hard because they know they'll get paid no matter what they do and because the final report will make whatever solution they come up with so complex and so confusing that no one will understand it anyway.

✻ ✻ ✻

An Enron accountant named Nancy
Constructed financial books fancy
When transactions offshore
Her boss chose to ignore
And made all the auditors antsy

✻ ✻ ✻

Q.   How many Enron accountants does it take to change a light bulb?

A.   How many do you need it to be?

✻ ✻ ✻

Enron CONFIDENTIAL:

Top Secret Offshore Partnership Development Process

1. Think up weird partnership name.
2. Select Internal Managing Partner.
3. Pay managing partner huge sign on bonus. Charge to partnership.
4. Select management team.
5. Sell management team huge carried interest in partnership for next to nothing.
6. Select business opportunity.
7. Find suitable partners in offshore location (preferably one with limited extradition laws).
8. Use Accenture consultants to develop incredibly complex pro-forma financial model. Charge to partnership.
9. Get financial model approved by Arthur Andersen auditors. Ignore conflict of interest implications.
10. Commence operations.
11. Pay additional huge amount of money to consultants to review business model. Charge to partnership.
12. Restate operating results into pro-forma operating results by using better of a) reality or b) what we really need to meet street expectations.
13. Accelerate anything that looks like it might be a profit into current Enron earnings.
14. Charge anything that looks like it might be a liability to partnership to keep it off Enron balance sheet.
15. If necessary, use consultants to convince auditors that GAAP rules are not necessarily applicable to this particular partnership. Ignore conflict of interest implications.
16. Pay managing partner and management team huge bonuses. Charge to partnership.
17. Continue to operate as long as possible.
18. Replicate model as often as possible.

✳ ✳ ✳

An Arthur Andersen auditor dies and arrives in Hell, where Satan growls, "Wait here while I drop these other sinners into the pit! Feel free to look around. When I come back you'll have to chose a room in which to spend all of eternity."

After Satan leaves the terrified auditor gets up and peeks behind a door with the number "ONE" painted on it in blood and sees auditors knee deep in boiling oil agonizingly trying to organize millions of ledgers, checks, receipts and other slips of paper into a GAAP compliant audit using nothing but calculators and old Apple II's with small screens, broken keyboards and Visicalc.

Horrified, the auditor moves down the hall and peeks behind a door with a big red "TWO" on it, only to see another group of auditors attempting to double check huge stacks of ledger postings while being scratched and bitten by a pack of small, porcine demons with razor sharp teeth and claws.

Barely able to contain his terror, the auditor moves further down the hall and with trepidation peeks behind a door with no number on it. To his surprise, he sees an auditor seated in a luxurious leather chair at the head of a polished conference table. Even stranger, he's surrounded by a client company CFO and a bevy of fawning client staff accountants who are offering him a variety of cigars, snacks, and fine wines while hanging on his every word and telling him how his valuable insight and financial genius are going to make this audit report a truly useful tool for shareholders and management alike.

At last, Satan returned and asked, "OK, times up. Choose. Which door will it be?"

The auditor quickly pointed to the unnumbered door.

"You can't have that door," replied Satan with an amused snort. "That's part of CFO Hell."

✳ ✳ ✳

An Enron accountant dies and upon arriving at the Pearly Gates is informed by Saint Peter that he must spend 10 years in purgatory before he will be allowed into Heaven. However, he does get to choose between Enron accountant purgatory and Arthur Andersen auditor purgatory.

"What's the difference?" asked the curious accountant.

"Well," replied Saint Peter, "In Enron accountant purgatory each day demons tie you to a stake, soak you in gasoline, light you on fire with a match and you burn for the next 12 hours. Then you get to rest for the next 12 hours. In Arthur Andersen auditor purgatory you wait around for 12 hours for the accountants to burn then the demons tie you to a stake, soak you in gasoline, light you on fire with a match and you burn for the next 12 hours."

"Doesn't sound like much of a difference."

"If I were you," counseled Saint Peter, "I'd take Enron accountant purgatory. The ropes tend to break, the stake is easy to pull out of the ground and somebody usually forgets the gasoline or the matches."

✳ ✳ ✳

A balloonist was up on a cross-country flight across southern Texas. Unfortunately, when the wind veered he was blown off course and forced to land out in the country. He found himself in an open field with no idea of where he was. Fortunately, a car was coming down a nearby road and he flagged it down. The balloonist asked the driver, "Can you please tell me where I am?"

"Yes, of course", said the driver. "It's obvious that this wind has blown your balloon off course. You have just landed in the south field of a private ranch owned by the Ramsey family. The ranch is 16.25 miles from Pasadena, Texas and it is 11,227.5 acres in total size. The Ramseys run 800 head of prime longhorn cattle on this particular field. Also, there is a very aggressive bull in the field and he is charging you RIGHT NOW!!"

Just at that moment the bull lunged and flipped the balloonist over the fence. Fortunately, while a little banged up he was not seriously hurt. As he got up and dusted himself off he asked the driver, "So, how long were you an Enron accountant?"

"That's amazing!!" said the driver, taken aback, "You're right. I did work in accounting at Enron. How did you know that?"

"I dealt with Enron accounting all the time," replied the balloonist. "The information you gave me was detailed, precise and accurate. Most of it was useless or redundant and by the time you got to the critical information I really needed it was too late to be of any help."

"So, how long were you in Enron senior management?" retorted the accountant.

Now it was the balloonist's turn to be surprised. "Unbelievable!! I was an Enron senior manager. How could you possibly know that?"

"Because you didn't know where you were going, you still don't know where you are and you expect me to be able to help! So, you're just as lost as you were before we met but now you think it's all my fault!"

✳ ✳ ✳

Q.   What's a good weight for an Enron accountant or an Arthur Andersen auditor?

A.   About 12 pounds, including the urn.

✳ ✳ ✳

Returning from a visit to Enron headquarters in Houston, the coach cabin for the flight was overbooked so the Arthur Andersen auditor got a free upgrade to first class. During the flight the first class passengers were given a gourmet meal with big, warm fudge brownies for desert. Too full to eat another bite, the auditor decided to take a couple of the brownies for later. Not having anything handy in which to wrap them, he stuffed them into the motion sickness bag from the seat pocket in front of him.

After the plane landed, when he got up to leave carrying the bulging barf bag, a stewardess approached.

"Sir," she asked, "Would you like me to dispose of that for you?"

"No thanks," replied the auditor, "I'm saving it for my kids."

✳ ✳ ✳

A visitor to an island inhabited by cannibals comes into the village where there are a number of butcher shops, each specializing in a specific human organ. He stops at one shop which specializes in human brains from various finance officers priced according to the source. The price list on the shop wall reads:

Federal reserve trustee brains	$12/lb.
Wall Street tax specialist brains	$15/lb.
Chartered accountant brains	$18/lb.
CPA brains	$18/lb.
Arthur Andersen Auditor brains	$110/lb.
Enron Accountant brains	$125/lb.

Upon reading the prices, the traveler asked, "What makes those auditor's and accountant's brains so expensive?"

"Are you kidding?" replied the cannibal, "Do you have any idea how hard it is to trap enough auditors and accountants to get a pound of brains? Besides, their brains are weird - no memory."

"By the way, does anybody around here have any Enron lawyer's brains?"

"No. Nobody is willing to clean them!" replied the cannibal.

✳ ✳ ✳

Q.   How many Sherron Watkins does it take to change a light bulb?

A.   None. She just remembers that she sent Ken Lay a memo about it six months before the bulb went out.

✳ ✳ ✳

10 Signs your Arthur Andersen auditor has completely lost it:

10. Responds, "Hah! Wouldn't you like to know?" to all questions.

9. Grabs your crotch to check if you're wearing a wire.

8. Keeps asking you if this is a test.

7. Makes it clear that "double entry" is not just for ledgers anymore.

6. Keeps muttering about "credible deniability."

5. Wants to know if you'd like to go with him to visit some of the offshore partnerships.

4. Asks if you know a good attorney.

3. You realize the drooling you're hearing on the phone is not coming from a pet bulldog.

2. Insists you sign a non-disclosure agreement before he'll talk with you.

1. Hints that you need a bigger paper shredder.

✳ ✳ ✳

An Enron accountant had a winter condo in the Rocky Mountains. Every winter he'd invite different friends up to the condo to spend a week or two. After the Enron bankruptcy he saw no reason to change the tradition so late that winter he invited a visiting Czechoslovakian accountant to stay with him. They had a great vacation in the mountains - rising early, skiing and enjoying the winter sports.

Early one morning they went out cross-country skiing. Unfortunately, as they skied around the corner of a large clump of trees, they ran right into two huge bears hungry from hibernating. The accountant dashed for cover but his Czech friend wasn't so lucky. He got tangled up in his skis, fell down and the male bear pounced on him and swallowed him whole.

The accountant skied like a maniac into town as fast has he could and found the sheriff. Hearing the accountant's breathless story, the sheriff grabbed his rifle and dashed back to the woods with the accountant. Sure enough, both bears were still there. "He's in that one, the big one, the male!" screamed the accountant, pointing to the huge male bear.

The sheriff looked at both bears, took careful aim and shot the female bear right between the eyes. "You shot the wrong bear!!!" screamed the accountant, "My friend was swallowed by that one!"

"Yeah, right," said the sheriff, "And these days would <u>you</u> believe an Enron accountant who told you that the Czech was in the male?"

> At Enron shareholders now see
> Flaws where Fastow and audit agree.
> > When the audit took place,
> > It proved a disgrace;
> They agreed one plus one equaled three.

6.0   Politics and Politicians

Before the Enron collapse, then Republican National Committee Chairman Haley Barbour was working in his office when his secretary buzzed to inform him that he had two very important visitors waiting.

"Who are they?" asked Barbour.

"The Pope and Ken Lay," replied his secretary.

"Send in the Pope first," sighed Barbour, "I only have to kiss his ring."

✱ ✱ ✱

Enron To Be Investigated By Houston School Board.

Continued recusals leave local school board as last resort.

Houston, TX (AP) -- It was announced today that the investigation into the collapse of Enron would be transferred to the Houston District School Board in which the Enron corporate headquarters resides. The decision was announced by the Mayor of Houston on behalf of his office and the city council, both of which had recused themselves earlier in the week.

The mayor cited extensive campaign contributions and other significant conflicts of interest involving all the members of the city council as the reason for the recusal. "Hell, boy," said the Mayor, "These Enron folks have been mighty good to us for a mighty long time. Damned if we're going to be the ones to piss on their fire if you get my meaning."

This most recent recusal followed close on the heels of the simultaneous announcements whereby the Texas Senate and Texas House of Representatives had jointly ceded the investigation to the city of Houston. Due to Texas state ethics rules, all members of the House and Senate who had accepted campaign contributions from Enron have had to recuse themselves from voting on any matters pertaining to Enron. With no Senators and only four representatives able to vote, there were insufficient members to meet the quorum requirements of either of the houses. "Well, it just goes to show you," commented one member of the Texas Senate on the condition of anonymity, "Around here you pretty much rent the best government you can afford."

Earlier in the month both the U.S. Senate and U.S. House of Representatives had ceded investigation of Enron back to Texas when it was discovered that only three Senators and fourteen U.S. Representatives had not accepted money from Enron. "Hell, we didn't even have enough House of Representative votes for a committee quorum, let alone a floor vote," complained House minority leader Richard Gephardt (D-MO). "We knew they had spread around a lot of money but this is ridiculous. If I'd known how many others were getting contributions I'd have had to think about it twice before accepting mine."

In a prepared statement Etta Bookmeyer, the superintendent of Houston public schools, said that the school board would take its duty to investigate Enron very seriously. "Of course," she added, "First, we're going to need to check for any conflicts of interest. We'll need to see if any of our elected school board members have accepted cash contributions or other favors from Enron – and, of course, Enron employees still have a lot of children attending class in our schools."

Lone Star State legal scholars were divided on what would happen if the Houston school board ended up forced to recuse itself due to conflict of interest rules. While there was no precedent on point, the legal consensus appeared to be that responsibility for the investigation would then pass to the Houston High School Student Council.

10 Things Enron Executives Should Probably Not Do In Their Testimony Before Congress:

10. Present response using performance art.

9. Insist on right to trial by combat.

8. Begin any response with, "As a protest against the systematic and brutal oppression of women and minorities..."

7. Whine piteously, beg, cry, etc...

6. Espondray otay allway estionsquay inway Igpay Atinlay. ("Respond to all questions in Pig Latin.")

5. Leap up, slap committee chairman with gauntlet and challenge him to a duel.

4. Threaten to toss anthrax filled envelope into air conditioning vent.

3. Start talking in tongues.

2. Explode, implode or spontaneously combust.

1. Moon everyone in the room when finished.

At the height of a Congressional hearing on the collapse of Enron the outraged Senator attacked the former Enron executive testifying before the committee. "Isn't it true," bellowed the Senator, "That the votes of numerous Senators and members of the House of Representatives were purchased by Enron's political contributions?"

The witness just sat there staring out into space, as though he had not heard the question. "Isn't it true that vast political influence in both the House and Senate was purchased with Enron's money?" the Senator repeated.

The witness still did not respond. Finally, the Chairman of the committee leaned forward and said, "The witness is directed to answer the Senator's question."

"Oh," replied the startled witness said, "I'm sorry. I thought he was addressing the *members* of the committee."

An Enron executive was in Washington D.C. to personally drop off a contribution to a famous Senator. After being ushered into the Senator's private office the executive comes right to the point, "Senator, I'm here to give you a $50,000 contribution to your re-election campaign. When the time comes, I hope you'll remember where it came from."

The Senator asks his two senior assistants to come into the office.

"Guys, I just wanted you to be witnesses to this generous contribution from our friend here. Please see to that it gets deposited into the re-election fund."

Both assistants thank the Enron executive profusely for his support and leave the room with the contribution.

A few months later there is an important vote coming up on a bill in which Enron has a significant interest. The executive again visits his friend the Senator to see how he plans to vote.

"I'm still not sure how I'll be voting. It's a complicated issue." replied the Senator.

"I'd just like to remind you of our previous meeting," prodded the executive.

"What about it?" asked the Senator.

"Well," replied the executive, "On my last visit I gave you a $50,000 contribution on behalf of Enron. It was even witnessed by your two assistants. Surely you'll at least listen to our reasons for why we want you to vote 'yes' on the measure."

Without saying another word the Senator again asked his two assistants to come into the office.

"Guys," asked the Senator, "Have either of you ever seen this gentleman before? Have either of you ever seen him give me anything."

"Never," replied both assistants in unison.

"Thanks, guys, you can leave now," said the Senator.

After they have left the room the Enron executive is flabbergasted. "But...but... I did give it...to...them.....," he sputtered as he started to protest but was stopped by a wave of the Senator's hand.

"I know, I know," said the Senator with a smirk. "I just thought it was important for you to know the kind of assistants I have."

✳ ✳ ✳

After the Enron scandal broke Senate Majority leader Tom Daschle (D-S.D.) announced that he was going to introduce legislation creating a new permanent Senate committee. As part of its charter the Senate Stock Market Committee would have the responsibility to advise and consent on all of the stocks invested in by the U.S. Government as well as overseeing the stock market.

"But, Tom," pointed out Senator Gordon Smith (R-OR), "The U.S. government does not have any stock investments for the Senate to monitor."

"So why is that a problem?" snapped Daschle, "The Senate has an Intelligence Committee, doesn't it?"

✳ ✳ ✳

A heated exchange between a former Enron executive and a Senator during a Senate Finance Committee hearing on Enron:

Senator: "Did you conspire to defraud and deceive Enron shareholders?"

Enron executive: "No, Senator, I did not."

Senator: "You are aware that you are under oath?"

Enron executive: "Yes, I am, Senator."

Senator: "And you are aware of the penalties for perjury?"

Enron executive: "Yes, I am, Senator, and they're a hell of a lot less than the penalties for conspiracy and shareholder fraud."

✳ ✳ ✳

The Enron bagman - uh - *executive* was calling on a new Congressman to "pay" his respects by offering to give the Congressman a new car for his son.

"I'm sorry," said the shocked freshman Congressman, "I can't accept that. It would be like taking a bribe."

Thinking quickly, the experienced executive replied, "OK, fine. How about I sell the car to you for $20?"

Thinking for a moment, the politician replied, "OK, fine. When you put it that way, here's $40. Sell me one for my daughter, too!!"

✳ ✳ ✳

10 Things Enron Executives Should Probably Not Say In Response To Senate Committee Questions:

10. "You call *THAT* a question? How the hell did *you* ever get elected?"

9. "Anybody else as drunk as I am?"

8. "Please rephrase your question in the form of an answer..."

7. "I'm sorry Senator, I didn't say 'Simon says ask questions'. You're out."

6. "I'd love to answer that question but I've got a ferret in my shorts."

5. "You think that excuse was bad? Let me read this list of worse things I *could* have said..."

4. "I'm taking the fifth...and while we're at it could somebody please get me one."

3. "Anybody here besides me think it's about time for a break?"

2. "I could answer that question, but then I'd have to kill you."

1. "Excuse me Senator, don't I remember you from the last fund raiser?"

Senate Announces Scoring Rules For Enron Hearings

Olympics scoring controversy prompts publication of rules

Washington, D.C. (AP) -- The United States Senate today announced its rules for scoring witnesses testifying before Senate committees investigating the collapse of Enron. This is a new approach for the Senate which has traditionally relied on shouting and the ability to turn the witness' microphone on and off to score points during testimony.

"There has been a lot of commentary regarding these hearings," said Senate majority leader Tom Daschle, (D-S.D.), "To the effect that the only reason we're having them is political posturing. Nothing could be further from the truth and our new objective scoring system is going to prove that. We're going to ask hard questions and the witnesses had better have good answers."

Under the new system all questions will be scored on difficulty and all responses will be scored on substance by an independent panel of seven judges. The high and low scores will be eliminated and the five remaining scores averaged to produce the final score. The highest score would be 6.0 on both difficulty and substance. Taking the fifth will automatically result in a 0.0 score in both categories.

"We think using the difficulty and substance grades is important in assigning an overall score," continued Daschle. "After all, anybody should be able to get a 6.0 for substance on 1.0 difficulty questions like, 'State your name' or 'What state are you from?'. On the other hand, explaining a complex offshore partnership is probably a 5.5 for difficulty so even a completely bullshit answer, if sincere, is probably worth two or three substance points. Of the major Enron executives we've heard to date, based on scoring taped replays of the hearings it's pretty clear that Sherron Watkins has the lead with Jeffrey Skilling way back but in second place; Ken Lay is not really in the game."

Jeffrey Skilling, whose responses during his testimony were repeatedly interrupted by various Senators commented, "Hey, anything that gets those Senators to shut up so that the witness can actually answer a question would be an improvement."

Ken Lay commented, "I'd really like to make a comment because I have a lot to say but I regret to say that I have no comment."

Former President Bill Clinton commented, "I'm glad the Senate wasn't using this system when I was testifying during my impeachment hearings. That French judge looks hot – uh – tough. Who knows how I would have scored with her?"

The Senate scoring rules will apply to testimony before all Senate committees. The U.S. House of Representatives is expected to make a similar announcement regarding scoring testimony before its committees later today.

✳ ✳ ✳

During the height of the California energy crisis Governor Gray Davis decided to call Ken Lay to see if Enron and the State of California could work out better energy rates. Calling Ken's direct line, Governor Davis said, "Is Ken there? This is Gray Davis, Governor of California."

After a long pause, Mr. Lay's private secretary responded with sorrow in her voice, "I'm sorry, Governor Davis, but while there has been no public announcement yet, Mr. Lay passed away suddenly yesterday."

Ten minutes later, he called again, "Is Ken there? This is Gray Davis, Governor of California."

"As I told you earlier, Governor Davis," said the secretary, "Mr. Lay passed away yesterday."

Ten minutes later, he called again, "Is Ken there? This is Gray Davis, Governor of California."

"**LISTEN YOU INSENSITIVE JERK,**" screamed the secretary, losing her cool, "**I'VE TOLD YOU TWICE ALREADY THAT MR. LAY IS DEAD. GONE. DECEASED. NOT LIVING. KICKED THE BUCKET. GONE TO THE GREAT PERHAPS. BOUGHT THE FARM. SHUFFLED OFF THIS MORTAL COIL. PERMANENTLY UNAVAILABLE. WHICH WORDS DON'T YOU UNDERSTAND AND WHY DO YOU KEEP CALLING BACK??**"

"Well," replied Davis, "I just love to hear you say it."

✸ ✸ ✸

Ken Lay had just finished a particularly intense session before the Senate Commerce Committee investigating the Enron bankruptcy. On the steps of the Senate he stopped to address a waiting hoard of reporters, much to the horror of the corporate counsel, who had just noticed that Senator Tom Daschle (D-S.D.), the powerful majority leader of the Senate, was standing nearby and listening intently to every word of Lay's diatribe.

"These redundant committees are just grandstanding for the press and being completely unfair," railed the irate Lay. "They are a bunch of headline seeking twits and financial neophytes who have never been in business and who have no idea what they're talking about. Most of them are lawyers for God's sake – talk about disconnected from reality!! This whole thing is a complete waste of time and money. I deeply resent any implication that Enron lost money using anything other than completely legal means."

"You shouldn't take this too seriously," said the corporate counsel, sidling up to Senator Daschle and trying valiantly to regain control of the situation, "When he gets worked up like this Ken is sometimes really his own worst enemy."

"Not while I'm alive," replied the Senator.

7.0 Ken Lay and the Crew

Q. How many Ken Lays does it take to change a light bulb?

A. None. Ken Lay is always in the dark.

Q. You're trapped in an elevator with a crazed serial killer, Osama bin Laden and Ken Lay. Unfortunately, your gun only has two bullets. What do you do?

Pre-September 11, 2001 answer:

A. Save the company - shoot Ken Lay twice!!

Post September 11, 2001 answer:

A. Save the world - shoot Osama bin Laden twice then beat him some more with the gun butt.

Sign on the wall of Ken Lay's office:

If at first you don't succeed,

Destroy all evidence that you tried.

After spending a huge amount on lawyers and losing a large chunk of his remaining fortune in a vicious bear stock market correction, Ken Lay asked his wife, "Linda, if I lost all of my money and all of my power would you still love me?"

"Of course I would," replied Linda sweetly, "and I'd *miss* you, too."

* * *

SHREDDER MANUFACTURER NAMES LAY CEO

Manufacturer cites international experience, executive credentials as key to new position

Chicago, IL (AP) -- Shredtronics, the world's largest manufacturer of shredding equipment here today announced the appointment of Kenneth Lay, former CEO of Enron, as its new CEO. Lay replaces Vincent L. Canolloni III the current CEO who is retiring.

"When we saw Ken was available we just had to see if we could get him on our team," said Canolloni at the press conference announcing Lay's appointment. "How many times do we have a chance to hire a senior executive who has significant 'hands on' experience with our equipment? Most of the time the shredding is just done by office staff."

Shredtronics, which produces large industial shredders as well as paper shredders, leads the world in shredding technology. "Worldwide, I see this as a real growth opportunity," said Lay. "As you know, I have a lot of experience developing offshore partnerships. And it's not just about paper. These guys make equipment that can shred a Buick. Imagine the possibilities. You don't have to shred documents one at a time – hell, you can toss in the whole file cabinet. Saves a lot of time."

While growing steadily for years, Lay feels that the shredding business is poised for even more rapid growth.

"Eventually," said Lay, "People are going to wake up and realize that the 300 plus major bankrupcies to date that have resulted from the bursting of the so called 'Internet Bubble' have cost the public many, many times more than the losses caused by the collapse of Enron. And there is no end in sight as more of these flakey technology companies are still going down the tube every month. When Congress gets around looking into that debacle I forsee a sharp rise in the demand for our shredders – particularly in Silicon Valley."

When asked if he had any concerns about the controversy regarding Lay and the financial dealings between Enron and Arthur Andersen, its public accountants, Canolloni dismissed them as of no concern.

"Our accounting is pretty simple – it's all pretty much cash based. Besides," he said, "We're <u>very</u> privately held. My Grandfather, Vincenzo ('Vinnie Snips') Canolloni founded the company back during prohibition to help meet the disposal needs of certain friends of ours. We don't tell anything to anybody."

Kenny Boy

(parody lyrics to A Londonderry Aire, English traditional)

Oh, Kenny Boy the courts, the courts are calling
From Congress halls, and round the beltway wide.
The money's gone, subpoena's are a' falling
T'is ties to you, to you that I must hide.
But hold your tongue while Congress runs its sideshow
Or when the press guys question what I know.
'Cause I am here, inside the office Oval.
Oh, Kenny Boy, to pull this off I need you so!

But when they call and you are testifying,
When I am mum, as mum as Dick Cheney.
You they'll abuse, they'll say that you are lying.
A thankless task you have in covering for me.
And I shall lift not finger one to help you,
And twisting in the wind you well shall be.
Taking the fall, you'll be just like G. Liddy.
And Enron slips from sight with nothing stuck to me.

Tim Russert, Sam Donaldson and Ken Lay were en route to New York when the airplane in which they were flying crashed. Russert and Donaldson find themselves in the judgment hall of Purgatory, but Lay is nowhere to be seen. After an interminable wait, each in turn approaches the dais to hear his sentence.

"Tim Russert," a basso profundo voice boomed, "In penance for your sins you are required to spend the next 10 years doing travel features for *Dateline*; no political interviews, no controversial stories, no hard news."

"Sam Donaldson," the voice continued, "In penance for your sins you are required to spend the next 20 years doing restaurant reviews for *20/20*; no political interviews, no controversial stories, no hard news."

Leaving the judgment hall to begin their sentences, they notice Ken Lay in the adjoining hall handcuffed to Paula Zahn. As they are about to ask the docent what's going on they hear the familiar voice boom, "Paula Zahn, in penance for your sins...."

In the fall of 2001 Ken Lay was desperately running around trying to raise some additional cash to stave off Enron's eminent demise. In a final meeting with a group of bankers, Lay and his team presented an extensive list of all the collateral the company had for a new loan. There were energy contracts, accounts receivable, fixed assets, equity investments, partnership interests, etc. - an impressive collection - but the bankers told him it still wasn't quite enough to make them happy.

"Doesn't Enron own anything else that is fully paid for and that you can put up for additional collateral?" asked the head of the banking syndicate.

And Dick Cheney hasn't been seen or heard from since.

Ken Lay's post-departure personal choices for the Enron company song:

10. "The Impossible Dream"

9. "Both Sides Now"

8. "Ah yes, I remember it well"

7. "Won't get fooled again"

6. "Paint It Black"

5. "As I Gently Leave You"

4. "Bad Moon Rising"

3. "I Did It My Way"

2. "Enron, Enron Uber Alles"

1. "Once upon a time"

✳ ✳ ✳

Ken Lay, still rich in spite of the Enron collapse, decides to throw a grand party for his sixtieth birthday. During the party he grabs the microphone and announces to his guests that he has had the swimming pool stocked with two great white sharks and a couple hundred piranhas. "I will give my brand new Lamborghini to any person who has the courage to swim across that pool."

There are no takers so the party continues for a couple hours until suddenly there is a great splash down by the pool. When all the guests run to poolside to find out what has happened they see Sherron Watkins (who had secretly crashed the party) swimming as hard as she can for the far side of the pool. Fins are flashing, jaws are snapping and the water is frothing but Sherron just keeps on going. Just as the sharks are about to overtake her she reaches the far side of the pool and clambers out; tired and wet, with a few piranhas hanging off her she is otherwise unharmed.

Overwhelmed by this demonstration of skill and courage, Ken Lay again grabs the microphone and says, "I am a man of my word. Sherron, even though you ratted me and your fellow Enron executives out to Congress, in the press and on national TV, I am ready to give you the keys to my brand new Lamborghini for you are undoubtedly the bravest person I have ever seen."

Lay is still talking when Watkins grabs the microphone out of his hand and yells, "First let's find Andrew Fastow. HE'S THE ONE WHO SHOVED ME IN!"

✳ ✳ ✳

KEN LAY'S LIMERICK

A Enron tycoon name of Lay
Couldn't keep the Congress at bay
    Though questioned and prodded
    Throughout it he nodded
With answers but nothing to say.

✳ ✳ ✳

10 things you're not likely to hear Ken Lay say in public:

10. "Damn! I think I accidentally shredded my Diners Club card".

9. "You know, a month ago I couldn't even spell 'subpoena'."

8. "I miss my jet."

7. "Maybe I should have paid more attention to those memos from Sherron Watkins."

6. "Jesus, how much do you have to contribute to these guys to get some results?"

5. "Linda's TV appearance might not have been such a good idea."

4. "You'd think that Dick Cheney would at least return my phone calls."

3. "Boy, those guys at Accenture sure knew their stuff. NOT!!"

2. "Oh, yeah, like I should have waited until <u>after</u> all the bad news was out before I sold my stock! AS IF!!"

1. "Doesn't know me, eh? Wait until George W. sees <u>these</u> pictures!"

✳ ✳ ✳

While sailing his yacht solo in the Gulf of Texas, Ken Lay fell overboard a few miles from South Padre Island. After paddling around for a while in the gulf water he was picked up by a young man in a small sailboat.

Safely on board, Ken expressed his gratitude, "Thanks for saving me. I'm Ken Lay, Chairman of Enron, one of the world's most powerful men. Name a reward and it's yours."

Thinking for a minute, the young man replied, "I'd like to have a way cool funeral and afterwards a major party for all my friends."

Pondering the odd request, Ken asked for clarification, "A fancy funeral seems like a pretty random request for someone your age. Isn't there something else more appropriate that you want."

"Well," replied the young man, "It's just that my uncle lost a huge amount of money when Enron went in the tank and when he finds out that I saved you from drowning he's going to kill me!!"

✳ ✳ ✳

One afternoon, CEO Chuck Watson of Dynegy - an energy company locked in a bitter legal battle with Enron over a failed merger - was taking a break to walk around Hermann Park in Houston and regain his perspective when he happened upon an old brass lamp. Tarnished and covered with weeds and Spanish moss, the lamp had clearly seen better days. As he sat down on a log and began polishing the lamp there was suddenly a bright blue flash and a small, rotund genie bearing an uncanny resemblance to Karl Rove popped into view amid a swirl of acrid smoke.

"I am the genie of the lamp," said the genie, "And as your reward for liberating me I will grant you three wishes. You must choose now. Know ye, however, that this lamp was once the property of Ken Lay. Whatsoever you ask of me I am obligated to grant to him two fold."

After thinking for a few minutes, Watson responded, "For my first wish I want one billion dollars in my personal checking account."

"Your wish is my command. One billion dollars has been deposited in your personal checking account. Two billion dollars has also been deposited in Ken Lay's personal checking account."

"For my second wish," continued Watson, "When I arrive home I would like that red Ferrari 250 GTO that I have always wanted to be waiting for me in my driveway."

"Your wish is my command. The car you have wished for is now parked in the driveway at your home. Two red Ferraris are now parked in Ken Lay's driveway."

"For my third and final wish," said Watson, "I want you to listen very closely. I'm going to go from here to the nearest hospital. Once I'm safely there, I want to have a heart attack that exactly half kills me."

"Your wish is my command," replied the genie.

✳ ✳ ✳

Ken Lay dies and finds himself at the Pearly Gates. Saint Peter then informs Ken that he is just on the edge of good enough for Heaven or bad enough for Hell so he will be allowed to choose between spending an eternity in Heaven or in Hell. Lay, dead but no fool, asks if he can look around both places before making his final decision.

"Very well," says St. Peter. " Let's start with Hell."

There is immediately a flash and they are transported to the nether regions. When the smoke clears Ken is surprised to see beautiful beaches. A marimba band is playing in the background. There are gorgeous women in revealing swimsuits. A great buffet is laid out. He sees lots of his former friends from Enron chatting down by the pool. The place has all the trappings of a world class resort. "Very impressive," enthuses Lay, figuring that if this is Hell, the downside of being dead must be pretty limited. "Let's check out Heaven, now."

Another flash and they are transported back to the ethereal plane. A soft white light glows everywhere. There are discussion groups debating various aspects of theology. A heavenly choir singing joyous praises to God is heard continuously. Everyone is wearing comfortable unisex leisure suits. It looks and sounds like Oral Roberts University.

"No offense," says Ken after a moment of thought, "But based upon what I've seen I think I'll take Hell."

There is a final flash and Ken is stunned to find himself chained hip deep in a pool of molten lava while an unending line of former Enron employees, vendors, customers and stockholders line up to get their chance to inflict vicious paper cuts on him with an unending supply of Enron stock certificates.

When Ken screams in pain for help, Saint Peter re-appears.

"What's the problem?" asks Saint Peter.

"WHAT'S THE PROBLEM!!!" shrieks Ken. **"THIS ISN'T WHAT YOU SHOWED ME. WHERE IS THE POOL, THE BEACH, THE BUFFET, THE BABES????"**

"Ah," smiled Saint Peter, "Before you were a tourist. Now you're a resident."

✳ ✳ ✳

Ken Lay, Jeffrey Skilling and Andrew Fastow went out to lunch. While walking back by some new construction in downtown Houston they saw a dirty, dented brass lamp lying next to a recently dug trench. Curious, Fastow picked it up and gave it a rub. Instantly, there was a bright flash and a genie appeared. At first glance Lay thought that the genie looked decidedly like a blue tinted version of *Politically Incorrect's* Bill Maher but he was not really sure.

"OK, you all know the drill," said the genie, "Three wishes. But since there are three of you, I'm only going to let you have one wish each."

"Great!!" said Fastow. "Send me to Hawaii forever with a beautiful blonde."

POOF!! There was a bright flash of light, a puff of blue smoke and he was gone.

"Now me, Now me!!" said Skilling. "Send me to Tahiti forever with two beautiful blondes."

POOF!! As before, there was a bright flash of light, a puff of blue smoke and he was gone.

The genie then turned to Ken Lay. "OK, its your turn now. What do you want?"

Thinking a minute, Ken smiled, "I want those two back in their offices and working at their desks right now."

✳ ✳ ✳

Ken Lay awoke in a hospital bed after major surgery and found that the curtains in his hospital room were tightly drawn, darkening the room.

"Why are the curtains closed?" he asked the nurse.

The nurse replied, "There's a huge fire burning out of control in the building right across the street from your window. We were afraid that you might wake up, see all the smoke and flames and think that the operation had been unsuccessful."

✳ ✳ ✳

10 Things not to tell Ken Lay at the Enron Board meeting:

10. "Heard any good jokes, lately?"

9. "Margin call."

8. "The shredder repair guy is here."

7. "Hackers replaced our Internet home page with a link to Green Peace."

6. "Mike Wallace is in the lobby."

5. "Dick Cheney's office called and said the golf junket is off."

4. "Gray Davis asked you to call him ASAP."

3. "Where would you like this box of subpoenas?"

2. "John Ashcroft is calling on line 2."

1. "Your wife's lawyer is calling on line 1."

✳ ✳ ✳

While driving home from the Enron company Christmas party, Ken Lay and his wife were pulled over by a Houston policeman. After examining his driver's license and registration, the officer said to Ken, "Mr. Lay, do you realize that you were going over 70 mph in a 45 mph zone?"

"No way," replied Ken. "I don't think I was going over 60. Your radar must be out of calibration."

"Hah," said his wife Linda, unbidden. "My husband is a notorious speed demon. Everybody knows it. I think we were going over 80!"

Ken glares at her but keeps his cool.

"Also," continued the trooper, "Mr. Lay, I notice that you are not wearing your seat belt. That's an infraction here in Texas and I'm going to have to write you a ticket for that, too."

"Now wait a minute," said Ken, becoming a bit more agitated. "I just unbuckled the seat belt when you pulled us over so I could get out my wallet."

"What a liar," said Mrs. Lay. "He never wears his seat belt. I nag him about it all the time."

"GOD DAMN IT, LINDA," yelled Ken, losing it. **"WILL YOU PLEASE JUST SHUT UP AND LET ME HANDLE THIS!!!!"**

"Excuse me, Mrs. Lay," interrupted the trooper. "Is Mr. Lay always this verbally abusive to you?"

"Why no, officer," replied his wife with a wicked smile, "Only when he drinks."

After another fun week of congressional hearings Ken Lay was preparing to board a plane back to Houston when he heard that the Pope was on the same flight. "This is interesting," thought Ken. "I've always wanted to meet the Pope. Today I should be able to see him or maybe even talk to him in person."

Imagine Ken's surprise when the Holy Father sat down in the seat next to him for the flight. Shortly after takeoff, the Pope began a crossword puzzle. "This is fantastic," thought Ken. "I used to be pretty good at crossword puzzles. If he gets stuck maybe he'll ask me to help."

Sure enough, almost immediately the Pope turned to Lay and said, "Excuse me my son, but do you know a five letter word referring to a very unpleasant woman and that ends in the letters 'itch'?"

Only one word leapt to mind ... "Hmmm...," thought Ken, "I can't tell the Pope that. There must be another word." Lay wracked his brain for a while then it hit him. Triumphant, he turned to the Pope and said, "Your Holiness, I think the word you're looking for is 'witch'."

"Oooooh, of course!" replied the Pontiff. "Thank you my son. By the way, do you have an eraser?"

Q.   What do you need when you have Ken Lay and a group of Enron executives up to their necks in concrete?

A.   More concrete.

If Ken Lay and his team had been running the Sahara desert it would have run out of sand.

10 Ken Lay impulse purchase ideas:

10. Shredder cozy

9. Two more congressmen

8. Kevlar® boxer shorts

7. Copy of *Crime and Punishment*

6. Cliff Notes® for *Crime and Punishment*

5. Classics Illustrated® comic book of *Crime and Punishment*

4. Personal copy of Quickbooks®

3. "Missing You" card for George W. Bush

2. Sen. Peter Fitzgerald (R-IL) voodoo doll

1. "Wish You Were Here" card for Jeffrey Skilling

✳ ✳ ✳

Ken Lay, former Enron CFO Andrew Fastow and talk radio superstar Rush Limbaugh are shipwrecked and cast adrift in shark infested waters. Their small raft has drifted tantalizingly close to shore but the tide makes it impossible for them to paddle to the beach. There is no choice: they are going to have to swim for it or be swept out to sea and certain death.

Limbaugh decides to go first. Stripping down to his shorts, he gathers his strength waits until the sharks are on the far side of the boat and jumps into the water. The sharks turn to pursue but, having caught them by surprise, Rush puts on a surprising burst of speed and scrambles ashore just in time.

Fastow decides to go next. There is no fooling the sharks again, however, and as he jumps into the water there is a mad swirling as the sharks converge. Expecting to see him torn to shreds, Lay is amazed to see Fastow rise to the surface seated on one of the largest sharks who safely conveys him to shore.

Finally, it's Ken's turn. As he gets up in the boat, from the shore Will and Fastow are amazed to see the sharks line up together to form a bridge. Walking on sharks pressed fin to fin from boat to beach, Lay strolls ashore without so much as getting his feet wet. Safe on shore at last, they compare stories.

"I'm a strong swimmer," said Rush, "So I knew I had a good chance of making it. But why did the sharks help the two of you?"

Fastow looked at them both with a smile and answered, "Professional courtesy."

Lay in turn flashed a toothy grin and replied, "Family ties."

One final thought on Ken Lay and his Enron team...

A clear conscience is often the sign of a bad memory.

8.   BONUS CHAPTER – ENRON Late Night

Here are some of the best one liner "sound bites" about Enron from the press and late night TV comedians.

"Special Prosecutor Robert Ray released his independent report and - I'm not making this up - he concluded in his report that Bill Clinton lied about his affair with Monica Lewinsky. Ray has moved on to a new case and it's still early, but he thinks that there might be some problems with the books at Enron." - Jay Leno on *The Tonight Show*

"Former Enron CEO Jeffrey Skilling appeared before Congress. Do you think they even bothered swearing him in? Now he is denying he lied to Congress last week. He's saying it was just the liquor talking." - Jay Leno on *The Tonight Show*

"Are you getting a big kick out of the Enron scandal? I find this interesting that whenever a big crisis starts, people start showing up in church. So, Ken Lay shows up in church this weekend. Church officials are still looking for the collection plates" - David Letterman on *The Late Show with David Letterman*

"Vice President Cheney is on his way to the Middle East. This is called, 'Operation Avoid Enron Subpoena'." - Jay Leno on *The Tonight Show*

"Jim Shea was a big winner in the skeleton event. He's the first three-generation Olympian from the United States. Skeleton is a very fast sport. Shea said that the key to his victory was visualization - he visualized himself as an Enron share plummeting downward." - Jay Leno on *The Tonight Show*

"Mr. Lay wanted to call it Enteron, until they realized that was a biology term for the digestive tract. In hindsight, Enteron seems right for a company of such ungoverned appetites." - editorial in the *New York Times*

"This past Sunday, former Enron CEO Ken Lay went to a church in Houston. On the way out, a reporter asked him how he thought it was going to work out. Lay said, 'With God's help we'll get through it.' To which the Devil said, 'Hey, I thought we had a deal'." - Jay Leno on *The Tonight Show*

"Are you following this Enron story? Me, I don't know, I just can't get excited about a Washington scandal if there's no sex involved." - David Letterman on *The Late Show with David Letterman*

"A lot of Congressmen yesterday were upset when Kenneth Lay took the Fifth. Lay said it wasn't his fault. He had planned on testifying, but when Jeffrey Skilling testified, he took all the really good lies." - Jay Leno on *The Tonight Show*

"The White House is sending Vice President Dick Cheney to the Middle East this month. You get the feeling that President Bush's opinion of Cheney has changed since the Enron thing broke? You know a few weeks ago, all they would say about Cheney is that he was in a safe, undisclosed location. He's hidden away. As soon as Enron popped up, they sent him to the most dangerous place in the world" - Jay Leno on *The Tonight Show*

"In the Enron scandal, whistleblower Sherron Watkins is now calling herself Enron Brockovitch. She testified Ken Lay was duped by the other executives. Oh, yeah? When is the last time you got duped and made $100 million?" - Jay Leno on *The Tonight Show*

"You're perhaps the most accomplished confidence man since Charles Ponzi. I'd say you were a carnival barker, except that wouldn't be fair to carnival barkers." – Sen. Pete Fitzgerald (R-IL) in comments to Ken Lay at a U.S. Senate hearing.

"Today the United States admitted that after months and months of searching, we still have no idea where Osama bin Laden is. Osama bin Laden? We can't even find Ken Lay." - Jay Leno on *The Tonight Show*

"The Houston Astros want to change the name of Enron Field where they play. I guess the Enron name could cause problems for them. Like players could steal a base and then deny it." - Jay Leno on *The Tonight Show*

"There are reports that former Enron CEO Ken Lay is missing. And I'm thinking, has somebody checked Dick Cheney's pockets?" - David Letterman on *The Late Show with David Letterman*

"Since Lay didn't show up for the hearing on Monday, Congressman Gary Condit says he may quit now. Condit said today on the news, 'Look, the day I can't get a "Lay" in Congress, I'm outta here'." - Jay Leno on *The Tonight Show*

"Patriots kicker Adam Vinatieri got an invitation today from Congress. They want him to come to Washington to kick Kenneth Lay in the ass." - Jay Leno on *The Tonight Show*

"The Enron scandal continues. The U.S. Senate has announced they are going to subpoena Ken Lay and make him testify. Apparently Lay received the subpoena this morning and then, out of habit, immediately shredded it." - Conan O'Brien on *Late Night with Conan O'Brien*

"I did not have political relations with that man, Ken Lay." - Sen. Fritz Hollings (D-S.C.) referring to President George W. Bush distancing himself from the Enron debacle.

"The White House again refused to turn over discussions Vice President Cheney had with Enron officials over energy policy. Cheney said if he had to disclose every time some business donated a ton of money then came in to write its own policy to govern itself, he wouldn't get any work done." - Dennis Miller on *Dennis Miller Live*

"Well, the manhunt continues for that elusive evil mastermind, but I'm telling you Enron CEO Kenneth Lay remains at large." - David Letterman on *The Late Show with David Letterman*

"The wife of Enron CEO Kenneth Lay, Linda Lay, was on the 'Today' show yesterday. She said her husband is an honest, moral man who has done nothing wrong. And today Hillary Clinton said, 'You go, girl! ...' She went on to say they've lost all their money. Luckily, they've still got plenty of everybody else's." - Jay Leno on *The Tonight Show*

"It was cold today. I was rubbing my hands together more than Dick Cheney at an Enron payday." - Jay Leno on *The Tonight Show*

"Enron CEO Kenneth Lay has apparently just slipped across the border into Pakistan." - David Letterman on *The Late Show with David Letterman*

"It turns out Enron workers were not only shredding documents at work, they were having sex at work. Having sex and shredding documents. Those are two things you don't want to get mixed up." - Jay Leno on *The Tonight Show*

"People are still talking about President Bush's big State of the Enron, I mean, Union, speech." - Jay Leno on *The Tonight Show*

"Ken Lay's testimony before congress is being referred to as the story of 'take the money Enron'." - Bob Hirschfeld

"The big rumor going around is, we may begin bombing Iraq. Or, as the White House calls it, Operation Keep Enron Off The Front Page." - Jay Leno on *The Tonight Show*

"Dick Cheney finally responded today to demands that he reveal the details of the Enron meetings. This is what he said. He met with unnamed people, from unspecified companies, for an indeterminate amount of time at an undisclosed location. Thank God he cleared that up. I'm ready to move on."- Jay Leno on *The Tonight Show*

"Wouldn't it be great if all of Osama bin Laden's money was tied-up in Enron stock?" - Dennis Miller on *Dennis Miller Live*

"Enron is now officially out of the energy business. They are now in a new business: confetti." - Jay Leno on *The Tonight Show*

"Earlier today, Bush's cabinet told him that they had nothing to do with helping Enron. Bush had trouble swallowing that as well." - David Letterman on *The Late Show with David Letterman*

"Yesterday [February 13] was Fat Tuesday. With the Enron scandal going on, in Congress it was 'Big Fat Liar Tuesday'!" - Jay Leno on *The Tonight Show*

"Enron CEO Ken Lay has sold all of his Enron stock. I guess we all knew that. In fact, the only thing he owns now is the Bush administration." - David Letterman on *The Late Show with David Letterman*

"It may seem puzzling why Enron, a company dealing in natural gas, would hire the same lawyer who defended President Clinton. Actually it makes perfect sense - they are two clients interested in laying pipe." - Bob Hirschfeld

"The FBI announced today that they are now looking for Osama bin Laden's financial adviser. You think this guy is in demand? How good can he be? His top client is living in a cave and driving a donkey. It doesn't sound like he is getting the best return on his investments to me." - Jay Leno on *The Tonight Show*

"If only al Qaeda had invested all their money in Enron."- Bob Hirschfeld

"New York police say that drug dealers are selling a new deadly type of heroin named after Osama bin Laden. There is an even deadlier heroin than that called 'Enron'." - Conan O'Brien on *Late Night with Conan O'Brien*

"More papers have been found on the destruction of America - and that's just at Enron!" - Jay Leno on *The Tonight Show*

"Congrats to Steven Cooper. He is the new CEO of Enron. Hey, Steve, good gig! Nice going there!" - David Letterman on *The Late Show with David Letterman*

"Congress is now discussing ethics of business. This is the first time for many congressmen - not in business, but ethics!" - Jay Leno on *The Tonight Show*

"This Enron thing is getting deeper. I just hope this doesn't turn kids off to the wonderful world of accounting." - Jay Leno on *The Tonight Show*

"Enron has hired a new CEO. This new guy is supposedly good at rebuilding companies and turning them around. I think he's off to a bad start, though. Today he changed the name of Enron to K-mart." - Conan O'Brien on *Late Night with Conan O'Brien*

"Next week on 'Fear Factor' there will be a special episode where they lower Dick Cheney into a pit full of people asking questions about Enron." - Jay Leno on *The Tonight Show*

"Today I saw a former Enron executive at a street corner with a sign that said, "Will shred sign for food!" - Craig Kilborn on *The Late, Late Show with Craig Kilborn*

"Do you know what Ken Lay had for breakfast this morning? Shredded wheat!" - Jay Leno on *The Tonight Show*

"In Houston they have decided to change the name of Enron Field in wake of the company going bankrupt. The new name of the field will be 'Oh My God, We Are So Screwed! Field.'- Conan O'Brien on *Late Night with Conan O'Brien*

"Did you see that? That was a questionable call in the game between the Patriots and Raiders. Even the Enron executives were saying the Raiders got screwed." - Jay Leno on *The Tonight Show*

"One year ago today President Bush took the oath of office. Just one year ago Bush was considered dumb and the CEO of Enron was a genius." - Jay Leno on *The Tonight Show*

"Wall Street has suspended Enron sales. Why? Is there a mad rush to buy them at $0.68 per share?" - Jay Leno on *The Tonight Show*

"Lots of news on Enron CEO Kenneth Lay. Wasn't that Bill Clinton's Secret Service name?" - Jay Leno on *The Tonight Show*

"Enron executives said today that there is not a shred of evidence that they did anything wrong - of course, that's because they've shredded the evidence." - Jay Leno on *The Tonight Show*

"On Groundhog Day [Feb. 2], Dick Cheney came out from undisclosed location and saw his shadow. That means we have six more weeks of Enron." - Alan Dundes

✳ ✳ ✳

9.   Dramatis Personae

Names, titles and starting page number of items featuring the principal characters in this book:

Ashcroft, John	Attorney General, United States of America	82
Barbour, Haley	Former Chairman, Republican National Committee	61
Bfstplk, Joe	Jinxed character from *Li'l Abner* known for bringing bad luck	25
bin Laden, Osama	International terrorist	26, 71, 88, 90, 91
Bush, George W.	President, United States of America	10, 26, 85, 88, 89, 90, 91, 92
Capone, Al	Famous gangster	25
Cassandra	Greek prophetess of doom	25
Cavuto, Neil	Anchor and managing editor, Fox News Channel	35
Cheney, Richard	Vice-President, United States of America	26, 45, 46, 73 74, 77, 82, 87, 88, 89, 90, 92
Clinton, Bill	Former President, United States of America	69, 87, 91, 92
Clinton, Hillary	Member, United States Senate (D-N.Y.)	89
Crown, Thomas	Smooth, rich, fictional thief from *The Thomas Crown Affair*	25
Dangerfield, Rodney	Famous "No Respect" comedian	25
Daschle, Thomas	Majority leader, United States Senate (D-S.D.)	10, 65, 68, 70
Davis, Gray	Governor, State of California	69, 70, 82

Letterman, David	Host, *David Letterman Show*	87, 88, 89, 90, 91
Limbaugh, Rush	Famous political commentator and radio/TV personality	86
Maher, Bill	Host, *Politically Incorrect.* Comedian	81
Miller, Dennis	Host, *Dennis Miller Live* Comedian	89, 90
Mudd, Harord Fenton	Famous con man from *Star Trek*	25
O'Brien, Conan	Host, *Late Night with Conan O'Brien*	89, 91, 92
Ponzi, Charles	Financial con man famous for investor scam known by his name.	25, 88
Rove, Karl	Senior political advisor to George W. Bush	78
Russert, Tim	Famous TV Journalist, host *Meet the Press*	74
Skilling, Jeffrey	Former CEO, Enron Corporation	7, 21, 41, 43, 68, 80, 85, 87, 88
Smith, Gordon	Member, United States Senate (R-OR)	66
Wallace, Mike	Famous investigative TV Reporter, *60 Minutes*	82
Watkins, Sherron	VP Corporate Development, Enron Corporation	58, 68, 76, 77, 88
Watson, Charles	Chairman and CEO, Dynegy, Inc.	78
Zahn, Paula	CNN reporter/news anchor	74

✳ ✳ ✳

About the Editor

Tim Barry has been in and around the personal computer industry since 1974. Starting out as a semiconductor engineer at Fairchild Semiconductor, his career in Silicon Valley included a variety of positions in hardware/software product development, consulting and general management.

The holder of six patents; the author of four books plus numerous articles on the personal computer industry, the editor of over 50 computer books and a former *Infoworld* columnist, Mr. Barry was most recently President of UCI Web Group, Inc., an internationally recognized Internet professional services firm. He moved from Silicon Valley to southwest Washington in 1997 where he now consults, writes, serves on boards of directors and bores his friends with tales of the halcyon years of the personal computer industry. He founded Intelligent Technologies, Inc. in 1998 to develop and market products via the Internet.

The Totally Unauthorized Enron Joke Book™, is the third in his series of *Totally Unauthorized Joke Books™.* The first two, *The Totally Unauthorized Microsoft Joke Book™* and *The Totally Unauthorized Microsoft Joke Book™, 2nd Edition,* are collections of jokes, list, and other humorous material poking fun at Microsoft®, the world's largest software company. Titles currently in development include, *The Totally Unauthorized Political Joke Book™* and *The Totally Unauthorized Politically Incorrect Joke Book™.*